The
Ride of
My Life

The
Ride of
My Life

A   MEMOIR

Gerry Pencer

*It's been said that every story begins with an
arrival or a departure. This one begins with neither. Or
maybe it begins with both. That's because when you live on a
roller coaster, you never know if you're arriving or departing.
You're just riding the ride, the incredible ride.*

Inside My Head

I hear the hum of the drill, but I don't feel a thing as it enters the left side of my head, just above my ear. I'm lying here, on my back, on the operating table about to undergo a craniotomy to have my malignant brain tumor removed. This is one of the most difficult surgeries there is, and I'm going to be awake through the whole thing, which, you've got to believe me, isn't my idea. Actually, I expected to be a lot more afraid than I am. Anybody who knows me would think I'd be totally terrified right now. But I'm not the least bit frightened. My head is strapped into a harness to keep it stationary. I feel completely helpless, which I don't like one bit. It took the doctors and nurses a long time to get the fit right because my head is so big. They were joking that they might have to go to a veterinarian to find one used for a horse.

My surgeon, Mark Bernstein, is yacking away, as if we're two guys taking a shvitz. He tells me that the muscle running up the side of my jaw is so thick that he's worried about making the first incision. I guess that's what comes from doing deals on the phone twelve hours a day. Or maybe it has more to do with my lifetime love of food. If there's one part of my body that's had a daily workout, it's my jaw. A week ago I didn't know Bernstein existed, and now I'm lying awake with nothing but a couple of Valium between me and possible oblivion as he drills into my head. In the business world you usually take at least a few days to digest a major decision. But I put my faith in this guy instantly. I could have had anyone in the world operate. But I trusted him. He's Dr. Brain to me now.

Now he's inside my head. I'm waiting for some kind of explosion. Skin and bone and brain everywhere. But that doesn't happen. Dr. Brain is riddling me with questions. He needs to keep gauging my consciousness to make sure I remain lucid. The goal is to take out as much of the tumor as possible without damaging the surrounding tissue. One miscalculation and I could be blind, or paralyzed, or worse. I'm lucky my tumor is accessible. That means it can be removed without causing neurological damage. If it was located in grey matter or deep within my brain, they couldn't do a thing for me.

He wants to know about Cott. That's my company. If you read the business pages, you've probably heard of it. When I took over at Cott, nine years ago, in 1989, it was an unknown soft-drink manufacturer with market capitalization under $10 million. Now, it's the world's largest producer of retailer brand pop and it's worth over $1 billion. And it's made a lot of people very rich. Even if you've never heard of Cott, you've probably tasted or seen our products. We produce Sam's American Choice soft drinks for Wal-Mart and Safeway Select for Safeway. We do Sainsbury's cola in Britain. We do President's Choice drinks for Loblaw, Master Choice for A&P and Dominion, Virgin Cola for Richard Branson's Virgin Group in the U.K., private-label drinks for Wegmans and Kmart, and dozens more.

But what Cott did was bigger than money. We redefined an entire industry. We took on Coke and Pepsi and made them blink. And through it all, I was the tail wagging the dog. Because of us, a can of Coke or Pepsi costs less than it did ten years ago. *Fortune, Forbes, The Economist, USA Today* have all written big stories about the company and how it spearheaded a "private-label revolution" in the food industry. Harvard Business School wrote a couple of case studies about us.

I'm lying here thinking about thirty things at once, which is typical. I'm thinking about my family and friends in the waiting room. My beautiful wife, Nancy, and our kids, Stacey, Holly, and Clarke, and Stacey's husband, David Cynamon, whom I love like a son. My brothers, Sam and Bill, and their families are there too. So are Nancy's mother and her brothers and their wives. Her cousin Natalie and her good friend Barbara flew in from Montreal. Our old friends from Calgary, Larry and Baillie Shapiro, also are there. Great friends have gathered from all over. People who have known me during at least one of my many lives.

I've had many lives. My Toronto life, when I turned Cott into a comet. My Calgary life, when I turned a Honda dealership into Financial Trustco Capital Ltd., a $2-billion financial conglomerate. My life in Montreal, where I turned one gumball machine into the largest institutional caterer in the city.

I'm thinking about how I got here. How I've been down before. How I've always beat the odds. And how I'm going to pull it off again this time.

◆ ◆ ◆

The short version of how I ended up on this table begins on May 20, 1997, a Tuesday. The day started normally enough. I woke up at six-thirty, as usual. Actually, my trainer, Charlie Francis, woke me up for my workout. You've probably heard of Charlie. He trained the track star Ben Johnson, who won gold for Canada in the hundred-metre sprint at the Seoul Olympics in 1988. Then the medal was taken away after Ben tested positive for steroids after the race.

There was a big scandal, and Charlie became famous. He told a commission looking into the situation that his sprinters used drugs to keep them on a level playing field with the rest of the world. He was really candid about giving drugs to Johnson. "If I thought he could do it without drugs, why the hell would I have given him drugs in the first place?" he said. I like that. I like people who aren't afraid to tell the truth and shake up the status quo. They remind me of me. Anyway, Charlie got banned from training Olympic athletes by the Olympic Committee. Around two years ago I hired him as a trainer. And I lost about forty pounds.

Charlie wrote a book about his experiences that came out the same week Mike Milken went to jail. Mike's a friend of mine. He's another person who's been misunderstood. He did a lot of good for a lot of businesses, including a trust company I ran two lifetimes ago. But that story can wait for later. Charlie watched me as I walked a mile and a half on the treadmill. Then I leg-pressed I forget how many pounds. If I told you, you could count on it being an exaggeration. It was supposed to be four hundred pounds, which was an all-time high for me. I felt really good.

Then I went to work at my office on the Toronto waterfront. It's a beautiful place with big glass windows overlooking Lake Ontario. I was being interviewed in my office by an analyst who had flown in from Smith Barney, a brokerage house in New York. Then something very unusual happened. I couldn't pronounce the word *tertiary*. It happened again. I excused myself and went into the bathroom. I looked at my face and it looked the same as it always did. It was me, your typical cuddly fifty-two-year-old tycoon with a perpetually receding hairline and a salt-and-pepper beard. Then my chin started to twitch. I thought I was having a stroke. Now I'm the kind of guy who thinks he's having a heart attack when it's really just the smoked-meat sandwich I had for lunch. So I drank a glass of water, and called Nancy, who was in the office. Then we called for Barry Borden, Cott's doctor and a great guy. He said he couldn't see anything wrong but suggested we talk to a specialist. Ten minutes later I was negotiating a $300-million acquisition for a soft drink company in England and had pretty much forgotten about it.

The next day we saw Dr. Allan Gordon, a neurologist at Mount Sinai Hospital. He didn't seem too worried but recommended I get a CAT scan. We set one up for Friday at Mount Sinai. I've been on the board of directors there for years. After the scan on Friday, the radiologist took a long time to see me. Too long. When he finally came out, he looked grim. I demanded that he tell me what the scan revealed. I knew radiologists aren't supposed to provide diagnoses, but I'm not one to wait the weekend to find out what's going on. He shook his head. "It's really ugly," he said. He told me I had a brain tumor. A lot of things began falling into place. For a few months, I had been bothered by the smell of the big bouquets of fresh flowers Nancy likes to keep in the house. That was a symptom.

He sent us down to the emergency ward at Western Hospital so that the neurosurgery resident could confirm the CAT scan and give me a chest X-ray. I knew in my heart then that this tumor was malignant, though that couldn't be confirmed until the next Monday. That's when I would have an MRI (magnetic resonance imaging), which provides a more accurate view of the situation. After I would meet with Mark Bernstein, a neurosurgeon at Toronto Hospital.

I had the MRI at eight on Monday morning. Before I left for the hospital, my family formed a circle around me and held hands and prayed. My brothers were there too. It was crazy, but it also was comforting somehow. At ten o'clock I met with Dr. Bernstein in his office. He had talked with his team, who had seen me on Friday, and he had studied the MRI. Nancy and I held hands. We've been married thirty years and have had our share of challenges. But nothing like this.

What he had to say couldn't be much bleaker. He told me I had a grade IV glioblastoma multiforme the size of a golfball just behind my left ear. I found out that a glioblastoma, or GBM, as doctors call it, is the most common and severe type of primary brain tumor. They come in four grades: I and II are benign; III and IV are malignant and tend to be fast growing. One of these things can grow from the size of a peanut to a tennis ball in two months. I asked if I could die from it. I figured at worst he'd tell me I had five years to live. Instead he started throwing out odds at me like some bookie. My chance of living a year, he told me, was 90 per cent; two years, 60 per cent; three years... you do the math.

He was straight with me. I liked that. But he wasn't very optimistic. No one has ever been "cured," he said. With a grade III you can live five years. Grade IV means that you have to be aggressive early on.

In that nanosecond my whole life changed. Things had been going so well for me. Then this. I'm only fifty-two. It's strange. I've never had health problems. Well, there were those two kidney stones. And the gall-bladder surgery I had when I was thirty-five. But other than that, I've had nothing. Other than the inflammatory bowel disease that I suffered from for a long time, but it never required surgery. I have a little high blood pressure. And I have a little bit of depression, for which I've been taking Prozac for almost ten years now. Oh, I forgot about the diabetes. I've got a little diabetes. That was diagnosed a year and a half ago. But I still love to eat sweets.

The second after he gives me these statistics, the real Gerry kicks into gear. I'm thinking, he may know my MRI intimately, but he doesn't know who he's dealing with. He probably thinks that statistics matter to me. They don't.

So I start casing the situation. The first thing that strikes me is the failure mindset of the medical world. As good as he was, and as much as I respected him and was dependent on him, I knew that. To him I'm just another brain tumor. These guys want to turn me into a statistic, part of their protocol. They want to treat me the way they have treated every other failed case before me. All of the cases that make up their statistics. Why the hell should I accept that? I've lived my life beating the odds, and I've never shied away from a fight. Maybe this is just a reminder that nobody is infallible, even an omnipotent guy like me. This definitely is my biggest fight yet. I'll have to fly through windows. But if anyone can do it, I can.

My surgery was scheduled for Thursday. And that's how I got to be lying here.

Before I know it, the operation is over. When it was clear it had been a success, my office sent out a press release that was picked up by the Bloomberg News Service, which sent it all over North America. There were about thirty people in my hospital room crowded around my bed. Someone ordered out for Chinese. It was like a party.

I couldn't wait to go home. I walked out six hours after the surgery with bandages around my head like a maharaja. I had a bag of potato chips in one hand and a carton of dumplings and a big black stuffed teddy bear brought by Robert Bras, who runs Menu Foods, a private-label pet-food company that Cott has an interest in. I carried a can of cola in another. Everyone followed me; I was like a mother duck leading her chicks. My next life was about to begin.

As soon as I was diagnosed I knew that I was embarking on

a renaissance. I've lived my life with an unfailing instinct for opportunity. And I believe this tumor presents me with another one. Not very many people would see it that way, I know. But that's just the way I am.

I knew immediately that after spending thirty years in business, it was time for a change, to do new things, to learn new things, even though right now I don't know exactly what that means. I knew for one thing that I wanted to write this book, even though I've never written two words in my life. When I was at Financial Trustco, the trust company I grew from next to nothing into a $2-billion operation, there was an investment banker I worked with named Libby Leonard who gave me a book called *All I Know about Sex, by Gerry Pencer*. Inside there were two hundred blank pages. I thought that was hilarious. I don't even know exactly what my story is. My old friend Andy Sarlos, the Toronto money manager, once said that my life would make one hell of a Hollywood thriller.

Mark Benadiba, a great guy who started with me at Cott, has read *The Apprenticeship of Duddy Kravitz* by Mordecai Richler three times since he came to work with me. He says it's helped him to understand me. "You're Duddy," he says. He can't get over the similarities. I've never read it, even though a lot of people have compared him to me. But from what Mark's told me, he sounds like a small-time loser who wanted only to prove himself to his grandfather. That's not me. I need to prove myself to the world. I need to be accepted big time.

A few days after my surgery Benadiba gave me a journal to record my thoughts each day. I'm having trouble writing, but I don't care. I'm happy to be alive. So I'm forcing myself to jot down a few words a day. About my family, my life, my responses. My family isn't thrilled about my writing a book. I've had more than my share of notoriety. I don't know how to stay out of trouble. If there's some guy who's willing to drop his pants, it's me, I don't wait to see how things turn out. Ready, fire, aim. That's how I do things. But I have to write it, even if it ruffles a few feathers. I see this book as my legacy, for the good points and for the bad. About never being afraid to ride that roller coaster that's life. About never giving up. About never being afraid to take a chance. About turning your life around.

If my life has taught me anything, it's that what may seem to be the worst tragedy or mistake can turn out to have positive implications. That's why I can say that even with this diagnosis hanging over my head, I'm the luckiest guy in the world. I never dreamt that I'd do so well, that my kids would do so well.

I've lived one hundred years in fifty. So every day I get with my family now is an extra blessing. No one had a life that gave more fun. I've done everything I wanted to do. I have no regrets. There aren't many people who can say that. Well, maybe my only regret is that I might not see my other two children get married or the rest of my grandchildren. I've had so many victories and defeats. They're both important, because you don't enjoy the victories unless you understand defeat. Nothing had happened to me in half measures. Even the tumor I got was the worst. God has a special way of dealing with me: He always gives me a brilliant fight.

Maybe the average guy would sit down and say, Why me? But I figure if I could handle the other things that have been thrown my way over the last thirty years, I can handle this. Anyone who says these things are impossible to deal with is wrong. Nothing is impossible, nothing.

My First Life

My first life began at the Jewish General Hospital in Montreal on April 26, 1945. I was the youngest child of Harry and Clara Pencer. My brother Sam was twelve and my brother Bill was six when I was born. My mother had been counting on a girl. But out I came, defying expectations as usual.

My Hebrew name is Yaakov, for Jacob. My English name is Gerald Norman, but everybody who knows me longer than five minutes calls me Gerry. I was named after my mother's father, Jacob Bookman, who was a pocket-maker in the schmatta business in Montreal. Norman came from Naomi, my mother's mother. Both my mother's parents died before I was born, so I knew them only from pictures. My grandfather was a very nice-looking man who dressed well, always in a suit and a tie.

My mother, Clara, was born somewhere in Ukraine about 1912. We never knew her exact birthdate. She immigrated to Canada when she was nine years old, and she must have figured out a way to lose her accent because I don't remember her having one. My mom was a real lady, the person who kept the family together. She was nice-looking too.

My dad was born in the East End of London in 1911, and his family immigrated to Montreal a year later. He had three brothers and four sisters. His father's name was Sam, and he ran a newspaper stand at the corner of St. Lawrence and St. Catherine Street in downtown Montreal. My eldest brother was named after him. Originally my father's family was from Poland.

They moved to Wales to a town called Merthyr Tydfil. My grandfather was probably the first Jewish coalminer in the history of mankind. It's not exactly a job that a Jewish guy would pick for himself.

The family story was that my grandfather Sam died eating a tomato. I always wondered about that. When I was a kid, I liked to think he really had left this mortal coil in the midst of some kind of illicit act with two beautiful women. My father's mother's name was Dora. She was a devout monarchist. She had pictures of the royal family all over her little apartment. I was always afraid to go to visit her because she had a dog called Lucky who liked to bite me. My grandmother died when I was thirteen.

My parents met when they were both students at the Aberdeen School in Montreal. They fell in love and married young. My father went to school until he was fifteen, and then he went to work selling newspapers with my grandfather. My father's family was much crazier than my mother's family, which was large. My mother had two brothers and three sisters. Her family owned dry-cleaning shops. My uncle Issie had one on Côte des Neiges. I remember that his wife put plastic over all the furniture. And if my uncle and his son, my cousin Bernard, wanted to watch television they had to watch from the hallway. They needed a pole to turn the thing on and off.

I have another cousin, Harold Levy, who's the son of my mother's sister Celia. He is a nice guy, even though some people thought he was a bit of a character. Harold was in the import-export business. Once he told me a story about the night he played chauffeur for our cousin Bernard. Bernard had some kind of hot date and he told her he had a chauffeur. So he rounded up Harold, who had a broken-down car that was maybe twenty years old. And Harold dressed as the chauffeur, with the hat and everything, and went to pick up Bernard and his date. And he took the girl to this restaurant Le Reveillon, which is where I went with Nancy the night we met. It was a pretty fancy place. So Bernard went into the restaurant and he brought Harold, his chauffeur, with him. So the three of them ordered lobster and Champagne, whatever. It came time to pay the bill, and he called the chauffeur downstairs to the washroom and they realized that they hardly had any money. So you can figure out what they did. They left the hot date with the tab.

I was a real *mazik*, a little devil. When I was born, the family lived in a walk-up on Dollard Avenue in Outremont. One of my first memories is the milkman coming to deliver milk in his horse-drawn cart. When he went into a house, I'd jump into the truck and start to drive his cart down the street. Then out he'd come, yelling at me.

When I was three years old we moved to Cedar Crescent, on the other side of Westmount, near St. Joseph's Oratory. It was kind of a hotsy-totsy address, even though we didn't have the nicest house on the block. One of our neighbours was Jon Deitcher, who would go on to be a top salesman at Dominion Securities. He would figure in my life later.

I went to Lad and Lassie nursery school. My teacher's name was Miss Bone. My only really vivid memory from there is playing the triangle at a little concert. I remember concentrating so hard so I would ting it at the exact second.

After that I attended a parochial school called United Talmud Torah on St. Joseph Boulevard. Half the day was taught in Hebrew, the other half was English. That's when I became known as a mischief maker. In Grade 3, I had a teacher, Mr. Breadman, who would come with his violin to play Jewish songs on all the holidays. One morning, before he got to play, I took all the strings off his violin. That caused a real commotion.

The teachers in the parochial school had just no way of maintaining discipline. It was an old school with old plaster walls. The year I was in Grade 5, I dug a hole with a little chisel between room 19 and room 21 so I could switch seats with a friend of mine. I guess I wanted to confuse our teachers. I worked on it a little every day. When they figured out what was going on, my father had to come and pay something like $25 or $30 to repair the wall. That was a lot of money in those days. He wasn't happy about that. I guess that's why the school always appointed me monitor—to keep me out of the class. It was an easy job, running around between classes with messages and stuff.

My pranks were semi-harmless. I used to go down to the corner of Park and Laurier with my friends and sit on the steps of the City and District Savings Bank. It was known as the Jewish Bank. We'd take out our peashooters and aim at people's legs while they were climbing into the streetcar.

I also liked to take my friends up and down the escalators at St. Joseph's Oratory, looking for Brother André's heart. I was about nine years old at the time. We'd get to the top and the priests would come and chase us away.

I got into trouble, but it was never big trouble. My father got a kick out of all of these exploits, I think, which had a lot to do with the way I ended up. Most parents don't involve themselves with their children. But my father was a guy who really tried to encourage me. He never stifled my creativity, so to speak. He didn't care that I didn't like athletics. He never pushed me into doing anything, never burdened me with the kind of expectations that a lot of parents lay on their kids. My mother was not as amused by my pranks as my dad was, but I can only remember her supporting me. I don't recall her speaking to me harshly. I was very lucky to have the parents I had. Few people had the unconditional support and encouragement I had growing up.

I didn't mind going to school but I never studied. I was able to pass the tests based on my ability to figure things out. And maybe that became my model for life.

◆ ◆ ◆

My dad was my hero and my role model. I enjoyed spending time with him as much as with any friend that I had. He was very much the patriarch—everybody would phone him with their problems, just as they call me today. He was the person you went to when you found yourself in some hot spot.

He hated hypocrisy, just as I do. One time one of my cousins ended up in the slammer for something. I remember his mother phoning my father and speaking to him in Yiddish. She didn't care about my cousin, her poor son who was going to rot in jail. She was more concerned about the family name ending up in the paper. My dad used to make jokes about that. He had a tremendous reputation in Montreal as a leader, through the work he did in the community as well as the way he operated his business. He would take his last penny and be generous to both his immediate family and his extended family. He was a very, very giving kind of guy who would share everything that he had. I learned a lot from him. He was never strict with me and was very approachable. On the other hand, he could be a bit controlling to some people. People loved my dad. He's been dead fifteen years, but if you go to Montreal and ask anybody about Harry Pencer, everybody will remember him and how much fun he was.

My dad was a big-time storyteller, a joke teller. He was a legend. He was the supreme commander in a fraternal organization called the Knights of Pythias. These guys used to wear fezzes and medals and all this stuff. They did a lot of very good work for people. And my dad had a friend in this organization named Ben Deitch. He was a supreme potentate too. Deitch's son was a bit of a practical joker. One day he placed his father's obituary in the Montreal *Gazette* with the time and the place of the funeral. All the Pythians had to come to the funeral in full regalia. Here's my father and four hundred other guys all dressed in their fezzes, all their medals. And here's Deitch's son sitting in his car across the street, having a laugh. My father was amused by that one for a long time.

I was always my father's favourite, but he had a spot for each of his sons. When we were growing up, my brothers seemed so much older than me. By the time I was ten years old, my eldest brother, Sam, had married his wife, Judy, and was working with my dad. But he wasn't able to talk to my father the same way I could. If he ever swore in front of my parents, he'd get a slap on the side of the head.

My other brother, Bill, is also a different personality from me. His academic career didn't start off brilliantly. He enrolled in science at McGill and flunked first year twice, so he took off a year and started a lie detector company. It was the only one in Montreal. Birks, the major jewellery store in town, had a big robbery that turned out to be an inside job, and he ended up checking out the people in their store with his polygraph. Then he rolled up his sleeves and went to Sir George Williams University and got straight A's. He then applied and got into both Wharton and Harvard. He ended up going to Harvard and graduating with an M.B.A. My parents were very proud of that. He worked at the

Bank of Commerce for a short time and then he married Ida Steinberg in 1962, when I was seventeen. The Steinbergs were like Quebec royalty. They owned the biggest supermarket chain in the province. They were very nice people, and always very kind to my family. They're real class. Bill's wife is also very nice. She's a sex therapist today.

Bill ended up running the real estate business of Steinberg's, called Ivanhoe. Eventually he left and went into business on his own with a partner. Today he's one of the most successful private developers in Quebec. If you met Bill, you'd never believe he's my brother. He's a very introverted guy and very conservative. As a result, he's had trouble communicating with some people in the family, but he's very honest. You could trust him with anything.

◆　◆　◆

I think a big part of my wanting to have fun had to do with the fact that I was a porky kid the others kind of made fun of. Maybe becoming the clown was my way of dealing with them.

I got fat when I was seven. Until then, I was a little skinny runt. Then I had an operation to take out my tonsils and adenoids and I began to hemorrhage. I was in the hospital for about two weeks with all this cotton packing inside my mouth and couldn't eat. So my parents needed to fatten me up. My aunt Leah lived not far from the school, so my parents sent me to her house for lunch every day. Her job was to get me healthy. Her only son had been killed by a car. Her way of showing me love was to feed me. She turned lunch into a main meal. I started off with one meatball a day. In a couple of months I was up to twenty-six meatballs. I always had a few cents that my father gave me, so I would stop off at the delicatessen and buy a two-inch-thick bologna sandwich and a thirty-ounce bottle of a drink called Mammy. I'd sit at my desk and just drink it, much to my teacher's consternation.

Then I'd go home and eat another meal because that was when my mother cooked. She was a great old-fashioned Jewish chef. Everything she made was fried. Shoulder steak on Monday. Salmon cutlets on Tuesday. Hamburgers on Wednesday. The one constant in her cooking was lots of Mazola oil. There was always a two-gallon jug of it under the sink.

That's how I turned out to be rotund little Gerry. It wasn't the genes that I was born with. My brothers aren't fat at all. Food has always been a big part of my life. I even like to cook. When I was about eight I was home alone watching the Jackie Gleason show, which was live in those days. It was the episode when he flew through the air and actually broke his leg. While I was watching that, I was also cooking French fries in the kitchen. I got so wrapped up in the program that I forgot all about the fries. Before I knew it, the kitchen was in flames. I guess my parents had good insurance because they ended up with a more beautiful kitchen because of me.

My perseverance, I believe, came from my mother. When I was ten, she was diagnosed with breast cancer and had a mastectomy. She was only forty-two. But she fought back and lived for seventeen years after that. My father was a big part of her recovery. He forced her to learn how to drive a car and took her on business trips with him. They even learned to play golf. They had a lot of good times together, which is why, I think, she lived as long as she did. My parents had a very happy marriage. My mom gave my dad a lot of freedom. But there were times when she was sad, though I was too young to really appreciate it. She was a very loving person, but she had to put up with a lot with my father. He was a tough guy to handle.

Her sickness was intermittent, and that was very difficult for her as well. I remember listening to her cry at night. It was a really difficult time for her to go through. It seemed that each time she went into the hospital and we all feared the worst, she pulled off a miracle and got better.

I got the business gene from my father. He was a real entrepreneur, one of the hardest-working guys you'd ever meet. He taught me that you can succeed at whatever you set out to do if you want it badly enough. He also showed me that it's possible to fall down, dust yourself off, and get up again. His first business was a small trucking company that transported fruit from the United States. Then one of his people had an accident. His business turned out to be underinsured, so he had to give it up and start over again.

From there he went into the clothing business with Franklin Park Clothes, which was in the Burman Building on St. Lawrence Boulevard. They made the uniforms for Famous Players and United Artists movie theatres as well as men's suits. The suits always came with two pairs of pants. When I was a kid, I worked there on Saturday mornings. I remember cutting swatches of material. He always found things for me to do even though I was probably in the way. Then he owned a couple of Bond Clothing stores—one in Chicoutimi, Quebec, and one on St. Catherine Street in downtown Montreal. He did pretty well in that business. And he was in it for quite some time. And I don't know exactly what happened, but about the time I was twelve, things got tight. The family had to move from Cedar

Crescent to a duplex on Carleton Avenue near the Van Horne shopping centre.

It was a bit of a readjustment period. We lived there for two years, and I went to Northmount High School. I don't remember it as a particularly great time. I was on the junior football team. How I ended up on this team I have no idea. I was never an athletic kid. I don't know any Jewish guy who can climb a tree. The most strenuous game I played was throwing a penknife into the ground. Lots of my friends got nailed right in their foot playing that.

I probably made the team because I was the biggest and they needed me on the line to block. And my friends made a little fun of me. One day Allan Singerman with a couple of other friends called me and told me that there was a football practice. So I put on all my equipment to go down to the field. When I arrived I discovered it was a hoax. I was the only one wearing any of this stuff. I felt pretty lousy, even though they thought it was really funny.

◆ ◆ ◆

You could tell how things were going for my dad by the style of bar mitzvah he threw for his sons. He went all out for Sam's. It was at the Mount Royal Hotel and he hired a big band led by Joey Kane. I was not even two, so I didn't get invited. Then when it was time for Bill's bar mitzvah, all he had was a lunch. That's all my dad could afford for him. My bar mitzvah was another lunch. I remember it well. They served all the stuff I wish caterers would serve today but they don't because it kills people because of the high cholesterol.

Despite his strained financial circumstances, my dad always liked to be ahead of the pack. We were the first people in our neighbourhood to have a TV, in 1952. The first year, all there was to watch was snow and the CBC's Indian head test pattern but nobody minded. Having a television was such a novel thing. Then we got this huge aerial that could bring in a signal from Plattsburg, New York. I remember watching Rocky Marciano knock out Jersey Joe Walcott in the first round.

It was because of my father's need to take everything up a notch that Cott entered our lives. He sent my brothers and me to Camp Winnaukee on Lake Winnipesaukee, in Center Harbor, New Hampshire. It was the best summer camp, I think, in the United States. This was the camp of all camps. Even forty years ago, this place cost $600 a season. My dad had to stretch his last dime to afford that. I went every year from age seven till I was twelve. And it had all kinds of interesting people. The son of Richard Tucker, the famous tenor from the Metropolitan Opera, was in my bunk. Jeremy Reitman, of the family that owned the Reitman clothing chain, went there too.

The counsellors had to be university graduates. The chef was from the Waldorf-Astoria Hotel. I remember we had steak twice a week. The food was fantastic. The sports instructors were guys from Triple-A baseball teams or All-American basketball players. The only problem was that here I was, this short fat kid who couldn't do any sports, and I'm at a sports camp. I was ashamed to tell the other kids that I really couldn't do anything, so I told them that my sport was ice hockey and that I was a goalie. I spent most of my time hanging around the rifle range because it didn't require dexterity. I became pretty good at hitting targets.

There was a service station about five miles away from the camp on a dusty old road. And when the camp took outings, the bus would stop for fuel and the campers were allowed to buy a bottle of Cott pop, which cost a nickel. At that time Cott was bigger than Coke in New England. Its slogan was "It's Cott to Be Good" and it advertised itself with "17 heavenly flavors." The flavours were fantastic—things like lemon, orange, black raspberry, and black cherry, which was my favourite.

One thing the camp was pretty strict about was no candy. And parents were allowed to visit only once a summer. My brothers would ask my dad to sneak some pop into the camp. On the drive home from camp, we'd ask him to buy a case to bring back to Montreal. From that he got the idea to import it to Canada. So he struck a deal for the rights to sell Cott in Canada with Harry and Morris Silver, who ran an outfit called Silver Brothers in Manchester, New Hampshire. The Silvers bottled Cott in Manchester and Boston.

My dad began importing Cott in 1954, when I was nine. At the same time, he was running Franklin Park, his mail-order clothing business. I remember this huge trailer with "Cott" on the side backing into this narrow driveway at my dad's storehouse at St. Lawrence and Duluth. My brother Sam worked for my dad in those days. And they'd haul the crates up to the fourth floor, where they'd sit among the clothing. And then my brother and father would deliver them by car. Sam's first sale was to the Snowdon deli. My dad carved out the deal with Steinbergs.

My dad had a bit of the carney in him. At the circus in Montreal, he had elephants wearing banners, promoting two quarts of Cott for 29 cents. Cott was sold in a quart size rather than the twenty-eight-ounce everyone else was using. He always set up special Christmas and summer barbecue displays in supermarkets. Outside he'd offer kids a free ride on the Cott musical carousel with a purchase of a Cott beverage. And he would always be giving cases of the stuff away to his friends. That's just the kind of guy he was.

He really knew how to hustle. Pretty soon he had Cott sold at IGA, Steinbergs, Dominion, and A&P. There were always samples in the store, which is crucial if you want to get shoppers to taste something new. He introduced low-calorie drinks—seven and a half calories to the glass. He also sold fruit syrups for sundaes, raspberry waffle syrup, coffee syrup, pancake syrup, lemon juice, to soda fountains.

At that time, his clothing business had gone into receivership, or some form of it, and he needed something else to do. He had become friendly with the Silver brothers, and in 1959 they backed his purchase of Royal Stewart Bottling on Decarie in Montreal. The deal was that my dad could put X amount of money in the bottling operation every year. After doing this for a few years, he became a small shareholder, holding something like 18 per cent of the company. They were good partners for many years. Then the Silvers sold Cott in the U.S. to Great Northern Railway Company, which went bust not long afterwards. Eventually it ended up in Cadbury Schweppes hands.

Early on I learned that I had a real talent for negotiation, for encouraging others to share my targets. When I was a newspaper delivery boy in Grade 7, the Montreal *Gazette* ran a contest for selling the most subscriptions. The prize was a trip to Toronto for the Grey Cup. I really wanted to win. Not because I really cared about football, but I wanted to win, to be a winner. It was a huge route, so big that I'd never be able to handle it alone. So my father got up every morning at five and helped me deliver the newspapers in his car. He ended up selling half of the subscriptions. And I won.

I travelled by train to Toronto with the other winners. It was my first trip to the city. And that was a special Grey Cup too, played between the Winnipeg Blue Bombers and the Hamilton Tiger Cats. In a memorable "play," a fan (who turned out to be a well-known Toronto lawyer, now a judge) ran on the field and tripped a Hamilton player on his way to a touchdown.

We stayed at the Royal York, which was famous in Pencer family lore because of a cousin who was fond of going to Toronto and checking himself into the Royal York as Charles Bronfman. He ran up incredible bills—all kinds of hookers and food, everything you could imagine that he was ordering under Charles's name. He was a sad case. He was tall and enormously fat. He had surgery to have his stomach stapled and I don't know what happened, but his mind went even squirrellier. He became an opera singer. He had a great voice, and he got a few jobs singing opera. Finally justice prevailed and he ended up in jail.

When I was eleven, I started my first business. I bought some Cott soft drinks from my dad, and sold them at the Snowdon Fastball League in Montreal in Kent Park near our house after school and in the evening. Now that I think of it, I don't think I ever paid him back.

My next career move was packing groceries for Steinbergs. I did that for a year or so. I made 64 cents an hour. I don't know how I lasted even as a wrapper in the stores without getting turfed out because I'd always be clowning around.

My next job was at the Mama Mia Pizzeria on Côte St. Luc Road. I began in the basement cutting pepperoni. It was pretty grim down there. The only perk was that they gave me these enormous pizzas—at least four inches thick and all the pepperoni I could put on. I ate more of the stuff than I ever used for the pizzas. How I didn't die from indigestion I don't know. After a year I was promoted to pizza delivery even though I didn't have a driver's licence. I drove for them for about a year in these little mini pizza trucks with the ovens in the back.

About that time my dad's business started to improve, and we bought a house on Borden Avenue in Côte St. Luc. I went to Monklands High School for the last two years of high school and suddenly became the class jester again.

A lot of my adventures involved cars. I remember driving down Borden Avenue with my friend Sidney Drapkin in his father's Fury. Neither of us had a licence and we were too short even to see over the steering wheel. Then we saw a police cruiser and ducked so the cop wouldn't see us. So here's this car rolling down the street with no drivers. We stopped at the end of the street, where we just hit the curb. We were lucky that they didn't even notice that the car had no drivers.

I got my first driver's licence when I was fifteen, two years before you were eligible. My father helped me to forget what year I was born. That's all you needed to do in Quebec at that time. My first car was a little Hillman Minx my father bought me for $400. I used to take a bunch of kids to school. Just crammed them into the car. When I was sixteen I borrowed my dad's Oldsmobile convertible, which was a gigantic car. I'd take this car with the top down, and I'd park it in front of the diet doctor I used to go to. One day I was getting ready to get out of the car and forgot to look behind me. A car came by and took the entire door off.

After my job in pizza delivery I got a job as a curb-service waiter at Miss Montreal, a famous Montreal restaurant on Decarie. I wore a pillbox hat, a blue jacket with tails, and red pants. I was a sight. I used to stand outside and serve the house specialties—steak à la Dutch and fresh Orangeade.

I worked every day from five in the evening until one in the morning. It was a unique schedule for a high-school student who lived with his parents, who had plenty of money. But I just liked to work. I also wanted to buy a Corvette. I made more than $100 a week, which in those days was like a waiter today making $2,000 a week. That's how I was able to save up to buy the Corvette.

By then, I had made another career decision. I had decided that I wanted to go to pharmacy school. It was a real challenge for anybody to get into pharmacy school, so that turned me on. I also sensed opportunity, even though it was probably the most boring business in the world. Drugstores were independently owned at that time, usually by pharmacists. I figured that if someone could hook them up into a franchise, it would be a great business. Murray Koffler ended up doing it a few years later with Shoppers Drug Mart.

But if I wanted to start university when I was seventeen, I needed organic chemistry, so I got tutoring from the owner of a drugstore in the middle of Point St. Charles, which was a long way for me to travel. But the trip had a culinary benefit. You could get the best steamed hot dogs with special homemade sarsaparilla.

One night Alan Singerman showed up at Miss Montreal with his father in a big Toronado, a boat of a car. This car had power windows, and I don't know how this happened, but somehow the tray of food I was serving ended up inside the car on top of my friend. He thought it was a riot, but his father looked at me as though he wanted to shoot me.

One day I arrived at work to find a note on my locker from the owner of the restaurant. He was a really well-known restaurateur in Montreal. "Pencer," it said, "you're fat, you're sloppy, and you don't do a particularly good job on the curb, so you should shape up a little bit." His sentiments came as a big shock to me. I thought I was the best waiter he had. It ticked me off, to put it mildly. This fellow wasn't the most fastidious guy you'd ever meet. He used to patrol the kitchen and stick his fingers in every second smoked-meat sandwich or steal a few onions off a hot dog before it left the kitchen. I went back to him and I said, "Who do you think you are—Slim Jim?" I mean, this guy weighed about five hundred pounds. So he fired me on the spot. That was the end of my career as a waiter. Before I left, I said to him, "Someday I'm going to buy this place and fire you." And I did. But that's getting ahead of the story.

I couldn't not work after that. I ran a door-to-door Jewish catering business with my friend Sidney Drapkin for a while. We would get an order and get it from a caterer, pick it up, and deliver it to our customers on Friday. From that, we moved into gumball machines. I bought my first one with Sidney when I was seventeen and still in high school. Sidney's father was in business with a guy named Ronnie Bell, and we bought it from them. It was one of those glass bubbles mounted on a pedestal that popped out white, red, blue, and yellow balls of gum for a penny. We put the first one in a grocery store.

I called the business Associated Student Vendors. My capital was about 40 bucks. My dad co-signed a loan for a couple of thousand dollars so I could add more machines that dispensed peanuts, cashews, and little charms kids liked to sew on their beanies. The profit margin on gumball machines is incredibly high—about 40 to 50 per cent. Pretty soon we were earning $100 a week. The problem was that $50 worth of pennies weighed fifty pounds. And they all had to be rolled. My mother would help Sidney and me roll the pennies in the evening.

By this time I had been accepted in pharmacy at the

University of Montreal and was about to graduate from high school. That year I had a teacher by the name of Mary Dumbell (that really was her name). Miss Dumbell did not like Sidney and me too much. She thought we were troublemakers and kicked us out of class and told us there was really no need to come back to school for the balance of the year. She promised not to tell our parents as long as we just left her alone.

But I ended up having to go back because to everyone's surprise I got the highest mark in music in the province of Quebec. I had just seen a movie about Mozart and was able to ace the matriculation exam. The Protestant school board awarded me a $10 gift certificate for this achievement. It was given by the chairman of the board, Mr. Wagar, after whom they would later name a big high school in Montreal. Well, just as Mr. Wagar was handing me my diploma, he dropped dead. They had to close the drapes and remove him. I didn't know that he had died until a day or two later, when my mom told me.

My first encounter with a woman was not exactly like something out of *Splendor in the Grass*. I was fifteen and two of my friends and I decided we were sick of being virgins. So off we went to a woman we had heard about named Carmen who lived deep in the eastend of the city.

I got dressed up in my finest sports jacket. And just as I was leaving the house my mother cornered me and asked me where I was going. I told her I was going to the Hampstead Hop. It was the middle of winter on one of those damp, cold Montreal nights. So we got on the streetcar for a ride that took an eternity. Her place was a walk-up, a real dump. Outside her door there were six pairs of flying boots, which were these fur-lined boots with double zippers that every kid in Montreal wore in those days. It was like a conga line of these galoshes.

I was petrified. A little old man answered the door. We asked for Carmen. He didn't speak English, but he did know enough to understand her name and he ushered us in and he calls out for Carmen and we heard a woman saying, "Oui, Papa." Then Carmen walked down the stairs. I had no idea how old she was. She might have been forty years old or she might have been twenty, but to me she was very scary-looking.

After her first group left, it was our turn. I remember looking through a crack in the bedroom door with one of my travelling companions, who was only fourteen years old at the time. Were both peering in at the third member of the trio. But he never took his shorts off, so we didn't see very much. Then it was my first buddy's turn, but he couldn't do anything. Maybe he was too young. Finally Carmen got frustrated and she threw his $3 back at him.

As for my experience, I don't remember much about it. Her only English was "Three, please," which was her price, and "Are you finished?" The extent of my knowledge was a book titled *The Facts of Life and Love for Teenagers*. I didn't have a clue. All I recall is that it was over pretty fast. I couldn't wait to get out of there. I was in such a race that I forgot my sports jacket. I knew there was no way I could tell my mother. So I had to go all the way back by myself because my friends had gotten off the street-car. It was a really scary moment for me.

My first really inspired entrepreneurial effort had to do with wanting desperately to get laid. You have to understand the context here. I was 250 pounds. I was this horny little devil who had no success in finding women, and I couldn't afford the professional services I was obliged to consult. So I had to figure out a way to be happy and at the same time make them happy. I decided that my entrée with women could be a bust-enhancement cream. I'd offer them what they wanted in return for what I wanted. That's the essence of commerce.

So I took some Nivea cream and put it in a drugstore jar so it looked medicinal. The cream cost $10, which just happened to be this particular woman's going rate for companionship. The way I saw it, I was selling wish certificates. She was happy with the prospect of bigger breasts, and technically it was possible. It was a great trade. In return for my goods, she'd offer her service.

Obviously this thing couldn't work overnight. You needed at least a half a dozen treatments. After the fourth treatment, she began becoming impatient. "Pas grossé encore," she complained, which was French for "They're not bigger yet." "Mais Rome n'était pas batti dans une journée," I told her, which means "Rome wasn't built in a day." So this lady discontinued these services. I never found another customer.

The summer before I attended the University of Montreal, I took a little vacation to Florida with my friend Sidney in my Hillman Minx.

Sidney used to count the money for his father's gumball machine company. Sidney had saved up $700 in American quarters, which was a lot in those days. So we stopped at a gas station off the New Jersey Turnpike, and Sidney said to the guy, "Do you need some change?" The guy said, "Sure, I could use some. How much do you have?" Sidney revealed he had $700 in coin. So he said, "Come back after you've had lunch in the restaurant." So we got out of the restaurant and there were two state troopers waiting for us. They figured we had stolen the money. So they phoned Sidney's father, who had no idea Sidney had these quarters. Finally they let Sidney go.

We got to Florida, with the yellow light on all the way in this car. The first thing I wanted to do was visit a restaurant called the Noshery, which made these enormous desserts with thirty scoops of ice cream. So we rented two Vespa motor scooters. I was driving down Collins Avenue, the main drag, looking for this ice-cream place. I got to the narrowing in the road in front of the Fountainbleu Hotel and somebody cut me off. My motor scooter flew up in the air. I landed with a little concussion, and a broken left wrist. I remember a little old Jewish lady kind of hovered over me when I woke up, saying, "Sonny, don't you realize this is a dangerous thing for you to be doing?" I couldn't see straight. Finally the ambulance came and took me to the hospital and put a cast on, and that was the end of my adventure looking for the greatest sundae of all time.

I've lost track of Sidney. For a while he was married with a couple of kids. And all of a sudden he dropped out. Grew his hair down to here and nobody heard from him. But he came from a colourful family. His cousin Arnold was blown up later by a letter bomb. His father, Leonard, was infamous for his exploits. He used to send his wife to Miami for two months. And there was this stripper in a big club in Montreal. She gave him a life-size picture of her, and while his wife was out of town he hung it over the fireplace in the living room. And his wife came home early. The funnier story is another time that his wife was out of town he decided to show a porno movie. This was in the early days of the industry, when the male stars wore false moustaches.

Leonard liked to invite his friends over for a screening on his window blinds. The only problem was that the blinds weren't opaque, so he was broadcasting these images all over the neighbourhood.

◆　◆　◆

I was excited about going to the University of Montreal, but my career as a pharmacist ended in my first year. That was 1963, and French was the language of choice, which wasn't a problem for me. But one day I asked a question about botany in English. My professor responded in French. He said, "Quand j'etais à McGill, j'ai parlé l'anglais; ici, c'est le français," which means "When I was at McGill, I spoke English. Here it's French." That really burned me. I was totally immature—I had a couple of choice four-letter words for him and walked out.

I spent the rest of the year building my vending-machine business. Then I enrolled in commerce at Sir George Williams, which is Concordia today. I saw a big need for bulk-food supply and institutional catering. But that didn't last long either. I found the courses too boring. I'd be going to class here, going to class there, and I'd have one business here and one business there. It wasn't important to me.

My first management crisis occurred without my even knowing about it. I had one employee, a fairly recent immigrant, who was filling the machines. He was in his early twenties, a few years older than me. I was still living at home. I didn't even have my own phone. One night after I was asleep he called and my dad answered. He had landed up in jail and had no one else to call. This employee had gone to the hockey game at the Forum and ended up in the standing-room-only section. He got really

22

sexually excited between the periods and ruined the fur coat of the woman in front of him. My dad didn't wake me up. He went out to try and help this guy get off. I didn't even know about it for quite a while. My dad probably wanted to shelter me.

He rehabilitated himself. Everything turned out well. He became very successful. He came to Cott's annual meeting last year and I was really glad to see him.

Gumball King

Within a year or so, I had eight hundred bubble-gum machines all over the city. I kept buying more and more machines with the profits I was making. I had made money as a waiter. I had probably $1,000 or $2,000 from my bar mitzvah. That was big money in those days. But making money was never a big problem for me.

Then I expanded from peanut machines to full-scale vending machines. The first contract I had was the Veterans' Hospital in Montreal. I got that through Steve Herbert, who used to be a downstairs neighbour of my family's when we lived in Snowdon. His dad's name was Herbert T. Herbert. I always liked that. Anyway, Steve Herbert was a young kid who was an administrative executive at the Lakeshore General Hospital. He's done well for himself—went on to became the chief executive of the Royal Victoria Hospital in Montreal. Now he's the executive director at Baycrest Centre in Toronto. He gave me a break and let me install vending machines. The business grew nicely. For the first year or so, I had my first office on Metropolitan Boulevard, in Ville St. Michel. Then I moved to Alfred Street, where I had a little warehouse.

My first investment outside of the bubble-gum machines was a meat-pie factory. We sold meat pies to mobile snack trucks in Montreal. There was a big market for these things. My chief partner was Gaston LaMarsh, who was head of production. I'll never forget the sight of Mr. LaMarsh in this green sweater he wore day in and out for months. He never slept. You could see everything he ate on the front of that thing. He'd stand over this cauldron of meat sauce with a lit cigarette in his mouth, stirring away, dropping ashes into it. That must have been where the flavour came from.

For a time I think we were the largest meat-pie provider in Montreal. I used the money from the meat-pie factory to buy my first mobile canteen, which ran around the east end of Montreal, and I hired my first driver, named Cosimo Castracato, and I would go out every night figuring out how this thing was doing and how many of not only these products we were making but other products we were selling. I only had one truck and that really wasn't enough to build the business, so I went out of mobile catering.

◆ ◆ ◆

I met my wife, Nancy, in 1966. It was love at first sight. For me, anyway. By this time I had achieved a bit more polish with women. My vending business was going well. I drove a Corvette and liked to go to nice places. I had even had a serious girl-friend—a really nice girl named Rima Randolph. Her father worked for Suzy Shier in Montreal.

That had ended and I made a date with Ellen Singer, who worked at Kingsway Transport, where I had a contract. She said she had a friend named Nancy Halperin, who worked for a company in the personnel business. So I set her up with my friend Billy Schwartz. I borrowed my father's Continental because the four of us couldn't fit in my Corvette. And when I picked up Nancy, the first thing she said when she got into the back seat was "What a great car." That was Nancy. No pretence. Always enthusiastic about things.

She had auburn hair and very beautiful blue eyes and the kind of smile that could just break your heart. We went to see the movie *Our Man Flint*. I sat next to Nancy and told her jokes all the way through. Afterwards, we had dinner at Le Reveillon. The entire evening I was talking to her instead of Ellen, who was angry at Nancy after that.

I learned later that five or six years before we met we had both been on *Teen Time*, a local show in Montreal, on the same night. It was Montreal's answer to *American Bandstand*, and was on every week. There were two parts. The first part was a dance show and the second part was a quiz. I was on the quiz part, and came in second because I couldn't spell *irresistible*. Nancy was in the dance part.

The day after our date, my mother told me Nancy had called when I got home from work. It's something Nancy denies to this day. Of course I had to call her back. We made a date to go to the Orange Julep the next Thursday. Then she broke a date she had for Saturday night, which by coincidence was her twentieth birthday. I took her for dinner and dancing at the airport Hilton. My parents were out there for the evening as well. It was just the two of us after that. She would even help me go out and fill the vending machines. Within three months we were engaged.

I saw a lot of potential in Nancy. I really, really fell for her, but I also saw her as the perfect candidate for me to scoop under my wing. A month after we were going out I gave her $10 to dye her hair blond, just like my mother's. My mom used to tell me I was looking for a replacement for her, and maybe that was true. I really liked helping Nancy buy an outfit or two or to manage her finances. Well, she wasn't really good at it, so here I am, giving her advice, even though I wasn't that good at it either.

Nancy saw all the merits, or the demerits, of me at that

time. I was this funny-looking little balding entrepreneur, even though I wore a toupee in those days. I wasn't exactly Don Juan. Somehow, she fell in love with me. I think she saw me as the provider, the nurturer, long before I had any financial success. I told her she looked beautiful, that she was smart. She hadn't heard enough of that in her life. I guess this is part of the controller in me. I wanted to be not only her lover but her father too. I learned later that you have to let people bloom on their own.

Nancy grew up in a working-class part of Montreal. Her childhood was completely different from mine. Her father was very smart. He managed an office for Monarch Life, and he was good at what he did. But he was the exact opposite of me. He would come home every night at five-thirty for dinner, but he didn't have a close relationship with his kids. That was pretty normal, actually. A lot more normal than the way I was brought up.

One of the greatest enjoyments I had was teaching her about food. Her family were of modest means, and they rarely went out to eat. I introduced her to lobster and roast beef and all you can eat for $5.99. I'd found a very good restaurant in Saranac Lake, New York, and we used to drive two hundred miles there and back for the biggest roast-beef dinner you could find anywhere. Food was our life!

Her family didn't understand my family. One time they invited my father to dinner after my mom died. Nancy's mother is a nice woman, a really decent woman, but not exactly Julia Child in the kitchen. She used to make this gefilte fish that a cement mixer couldn't pick up. So my father shows up, and he slams down a bottle of Bromo-Seltzer on the table before dinner was served. That was his idea of a joke. And it was pretty funny.

But the Halperins weren't happy with that. It took some time to understand my dad's humour.

Nancy and her brothers are very close, and I've gotten close to them too. Mark was a partner at Goodman and Carr, and he's now vice-president and general counsel at Cott. He's been with us for about five years, and he does a great job. Steve is a senior partner at Goodman Phillips & Vineberg, and is widely regarded as one of the best securities and mergers and acquisitions lawyers today in Canada. He became a close friend and an adviser on every major deal I've done for almost twenty years and is a Cott director. I haven't always followed his advice, but I've always valued it.

Nan cy and I were married in Montreal on March 19, 1967, a year to the day we met, at the synagogue Chevra Kadisha. It was a beautiful wedding. About 350 people attended. But I was a nervous wreck. I signed Gerald N. Halperin on the marriage certificate. At the reception, our first dance was "The Shadow of Your Smile."

Arnold Drapkin, one of the ushers at my wedding, later got killed by a letter bomb. It was addressed to someone else, but he opened it. He was the cousin of my friend Sidney, with whom I owned my first gumball machine. I was friends with two cousins, and one of them lived next to me and the other one lived in a moderately higher-class place. They were in the cigarette-vending business and their family had been in it for many, many years, but I don't know what happened. Montreal could be a very tough place. They had nightclubs where they had all these machines, so maybe he put one in some nightclub and it belonged to someone else or something and the guy got angry. That's just how they did things.

Nancy and I went to San Juan, Puerto Rico, for our honeymoon. It took me about a day and a half for me to lose my spending money for my trip gambling, which was about $175. I had to phone my father to send me some money. Nancy was okay about it; she was always supportive. It was a lot of money for me in those days.

I lived with my parents until the day I got married. We rented a duplex on Gold Avenue and lived there for about two years. Then we bought a house in Beaconsfield on the West Island. Very few Jews lived in Beaconsfield back then. As I look back on it now, for us to move there was some kind of statement, I guess.

My parents' marriage was very similar to my marriage. Nancy's very much like my mother. And I'm very much like my dad was. And together we've built this thirty-year partnership much like my parents'. I'm nothing perfect, and for her to have put up with me for thirty years is beyond incredible.

In December 1966, just before Nancy and I got married, I was driving my Corvette down Metropolitan Boulevard and stopped in front of the Rolls-Royce head office. To this day I don't know why I stopped. Sheer instinct. I parked in the lot and went to the receptionist, and asked for the chief executive. I believe his name was Bud Mineaux. To my total surprise, he saw me. He asked me what he could do for me. I told him I wanted a shot at running the cafeteria in their plant. I explained that I felt that I could do a much better job than they were able to do with an outside contractor because I didn't have any overhead. I explained that I could work at a lower cost and would concentrate on serving better-tasting, less-institutional food than they were used to.

He was amazingly receptive. He probably thought I was an interesting crazy young kid. So he said to me, "Well, what kind of experience do you have in this business?" And of course I didn't have any whatsoever. I had no credibility. I had to make my credibility. That's what an entrepreneur does. So I had to think quickly. I told him I looked after food service at Steinbergs. That was a stretch, considering that the only food I managed at Steinbergs were the contents of my gumball dispensers in the stores.

I knew no one was going to hand me anything. I had to make it happen. Only losers wait for somebody else to give them something. They're paralyzed. Look at Donald Trump. Donald Trump did not succeed by waiting. Here's a guy who's a dreamer and he projects himself into his dream and makes it happen.

Mr. Mineaux was impressed. He said, "Great, I'm going to send Tony Coriglia, my head of office services, to go down there with you." So this Mr. Coriglia, who was a really nice guy, came down with me to the Steinbergs cafeteria. I marched him through the kitchen. And when I passed the steam table, I looked back at the menu board. I took out the tongs and saw that "we" were selling turkey and offered him some. Meanwhile, the whole crowd of the kitchen people are standing around me, asking themselves, "Who the hell is this guy?" But they were too shy to ask, and I didn't give them any opportunity. I knew we should get out of there in a hurry, which we did. I don't think to this day I ever told Mr. Coriglia the truth. My brother Bill, who is married to Ida Steinberg, never knew anything about it. He wouldn't have approved.

That became a template for how I operated. I visualized what I wanted to be true and made it happen. Most people would see that as misrepresentation. I call it potentializing. Most people aren't capable of seeing the subtlety of that.

We went back to the Rolls-Royce plant. And Mr. Coriglia offered a great report. But my trial wasn't over. The president asked me if I could cater his New Year's Eve party. I had never catered a cup of coffee. But that wasn't going to stop me. Just as I never take no for an answer, I never give it as one.

So I went home to my mother and explained what I had to do. The average mom would say, "What, are you—nuts? Why would you do this?" Not my mother. She sat down with me at the dining-room table and helped me figure out how to do it. She didn't know anything but Jewish food, so she suggested we go to a delicatessen, like the Brown Derby, and buy frozen hors d'oeuvres. She didn't understand this was just a bunch of WASPs who had never seen these kinds of things. She also suggested that I get her cleaning lady's son who worked at Macdonald College as a cook to come and help me to warm them up. She lent me the money, but then told my father she gave me half of that so he wouldn't know that I bought them retail instead of wholesale.

So that's what I did. I borrowed my father's tuxedo. Nancy waited for me in the car the entire night. It must have been twenty below zero. That's how devoted she is.

The party was a great success. There were about seventy-five people there. None of them had tasted Jewish hors d'oeuvres before. They went wild for these things. All these executives thought they were getting pâté, but they were getting chopped liver.

The cost to me was $200, but I charged them $125 because I had to make sure they'd think the price was attractive even though I bought the product retail. That's how I got my first big contract. Soon after I founded Maisonneuve Food Services Inc., which I named after the founder of Montreal. In a few years it would be the largest institutional and industrial food-service operation in Quebec.

31

♦ ♦ ♦

In 1967 I had a revelation. I realized that the government was taking all the silver out of our currency. So an old quarter wasn't worth 25 cents but 37 cents in terms of the value of the silver in it. So I took $8,000, put it aside, and went to find out whether it was legal to collect this silver. I was told it was kosher as long as you sold the currency to a coin dealer and didn't melt it down yourself.

I bought this car with very heavy-duty shock absorbers because we would have several thousand pounds of coins on board at most times. Every day my trusted lieutenant and I went and picked up anywhere from $8,000 to $10,000 a day in coins from hundreds of my food-vending machines, which by this time were all over the city, including at Expo 67. We took that money and sorted all the quarters, and actually dimes as well at that time, into rolls that were all pre-1967.

We built up a stake of almost $100,000. And after doing that for several months, I sent two of my vending-machine guys to deliver the silver to the coin dealer. Lo and behold, there were a couple of guys there who robbed them with machine guns. They tied one of my guys around a toilet bowl and took away all the money that we had made. Ironically I was left with the $8,000 that I started with that was still in the car. So it was bittersweet.

♦ ♦ ♦

The contract with Rolls-Royce operation led to others. Before long I was running the Trainman's Hotel for Canadian National Railways and Northern Electric's cafeteria. My days started at six in the morning and ended at eleven at night. I did a bit of everything—serving at the counter to filling in for the cook. Nancy helped out. It was a struggle. Pretty often I felt like giving it up.

Nancy became pregnant and had a miscarriage shortly after we were married. I was surprised with the sense of loss I felt. I cried when she told me. Not long after that she got pregnant with Stacey, our first-born. The night she went into labour, I was so nervous that I played a couple of show tunes on the Hammond organ. Nancy just waited for me patiently in the front hall. Stacey was born June 5, 1968, the night Robert Kennedy was assassinated. I was only twenty-three. In retrospect, I realize it took me time to understand what it was to be a good father. In the beginning I was too immature to accept the role.

For one thing, I was too busy working. I was only twenty-three, but I felt ten years older than kids who were my age. This was the 1960s, but I never smoked dope, or sat in someone's recreation room listening to music, or backpacked through Europe. Woodstock happened about this time, but I didn't have a clue what Woodstock was until fifteen years later.

I had kids my own age working for me. In the 1968–69 academic year I went after the contract for the cafeteria, vending machines, and coffee shop at McGill University. The operation was a mess. There were boycotts, huge deficits in previous years, and labour troubles. The food-services group there had no vision about food. Prices were high. The McGill Daily, the campus newspaper, made a lot of noise that the management had no choice but to throw these guys out. I gave a pitch to the student council promising pizza counters and delicatessens. I also told them their current provider was ripping them off. I promised to lower prices and eliminate management fees.

I hired students to help with the meal rush. We offered a 59-cent breakfast in the Grill Room—toast, juice, ham or bacon and eggs, and coffee. Dinner was 80 to 90 cents—things like veal marengo, egg rolls, soft ice cream, pizza, and fresh desserts. We lengthened the hours, put in an espresso machine, which was pretty exotic back then, and a jukebox. Any given day we were dispensing twenty-five thousand cups of coffee and serving six thousand full-course meals.

The McGill Daily was very powerful at that time. Anything they printed was like the gospel. I got to know some of the kids who ran it, who have gone on to a lot of success. There was Mark Starowicz, who's now an executive producer at the CBC. Robert Lantos and Victor Loewy, who went on to run Alliance Communications, the largest entertainment company in Canada, also worked for me, as did Norman Spector, who ended up running the Prime Minister's Office for Brian Mulroney and then became Canada's ambassador to Israel.

These kids were big shots around campus. They were the executives of the McGill Union at the time. I took every opportunity to make sure I had them working for me. You could say it was a training school for all these guys. I taught them how to run a business. They all had tremendous jobs. I trained these boys to help us launch a business in Man and His World in the summer. Lantos and Loewy were two of our most senior pizza guys. Maybe they were earning something like a buck an hour. But these guys now had positions of influence. They were able to give their friends jobs.

A lot of it was misinterpreted. Not in a major way, but there were these innuendoes in *The McGill Daily* the next year about why I gave certain people summer jobs. It was intimated that I did this in return for the contract. But that was a bunch of baloney. It's a big difference from paying people off. But in a way it's the biggest payoff. These boys were in business school. These guys got their M.B.A.'s from me. I potentialized their future and got work for me. By this time I was running six restaurants at Man and His World and needed to hire about one hundred people. Nancy helped me serve at the pizza stands.

The great thing about institutional catering is that it's a captive market; employees usually have to eat in the plant. But with McGill things were more competitive. Everybody else started bidding on it and we didn't have the purchasing power. The old caterer came back with a much better price. We just didn't have the ability to hold on to it and gave it up in the early 1970s.

By the time I was twenty-five, I had about 290 employees. We operated out of a ten-thousand-square-foot headquarters on St. Michel Boulevard. We were feeding about thirty thousand people a day. I just whipped the hell out of a company called Versa Foods that was really big in institutional catering, and much bigger than us.

I had about three hundred vending machines, but that was a nothing part of the business. About 40 per cent of that business was in universities. In addition to the McGill Student Union, we had every major university in Montreal as well as the University of Ottawa, and the CEGEPS, which are junior colleges in Quebec. We ran the Trainman's Hotel for the CNR and two or three operations for Northern Electric, IBM Canada, Rolls-Royce, Royal Bank. It didn't take long—I had hundreds of employees. I was even talking about expanding to Toronto. Our sales were $8 million to $10 million a year, but we weren't making much of a profit. It was time for something new. Nancy was pregnant with Holly, our second daughter.

My next move into the restaurant business was because of William Obront, who was the biggest purveyor of meat to restaurants in Montreal. Everybody bought from him—Les Halles, Ruby Foo's, everybody. I met Willie when I was no more than fourteen. His wife and her sister ran a summer place in Plattsburg, New York, that a lot of people from Montreal went to. My brother Sam rented a little cabin there. The Obronts were always nice, gentle people, at least to me.

When I went into catering, it only made sense that I would buy my product from Obie. The business he was in was a lot different from what we know as meat packing today. He used to buy cuts of beef from Western Canada, which would come on a big truck. Then he would butcher it and sell it to restaurants. He had the best quality and prices. He also gave the best terms. He was willing to support people who didn't have a lot of capital.

I bought from him as a commercial customer for some time. And he always gave me a fair product with a fair price. He probably gave me a little more credit than I deserved. That let me buy my merchandise and pay for it within thirty days. He was very helpful to a lot of people. But some of the people he helped out couldn't pay their bills, so he ended up with property or whatever they used as collateral. One was a place called Curly Joe's, which was right next to Joe's Steak House on Metcalfe Street in Montreal. It had been around since the 1930s and served good product, but it was never able to compete with Joe's next door.

Willie came to me one day and said, "I'm impressed with the way you run your business." He offered me a third of the restaurant if I'd manage it. He put up the money to do the renovations that were necessary. Our third partner was David Boltuc. His father had owned the restaurant originally.

Obront was a supplier, and he was exciting to a kid always

interested in walking on the edge. I knew there were allegations about some of Willie's business dealings, but nothing stuck. I never believed it. I think that it was all a bunch of baloney. But who knows?

Willie wasn't a tough guy himself. In fact, he seemed meek. He was not too tall, maybe five-eight, and he always had a very nice smile on his face. But he hung around with tough guys. He would meet with them or be seen eating with them. He held court in a restaurant called Schneider's Steak House, which was a little dump on Decarie Boulevard. I'm sure he owned part of it. He probably helped the guy to get it going. Sam Schneider was an immigrant who had a takeout place in the basement with the restaurant upstairs. He always had his shirt hanging out of his pants and he never shaved. He used to put tenderizer in his third-rate steaks to make them edible. Once he was preparing food for the High Holidays, and a little Jewish lady walked in to buy some stuff and she said, "Mr. Schneider, is your chopped liver fresh?" And he looks at her and says, "If it wasn't fresh, do you think I'd tell you?" What a schmendrick.

Willie would invite me the odd time for lunch at Schneider's to talk about how much he was going to raise or lower my rib-steak prices. They'd be these lavish lunches, with a bottle or two of Crown Royal on the table. These would be marathon sessions. They'd begin at noon and end around four. This was the old style. They'd just sit around talking about steaks and broads. Some of them would play cards in the back room.

There was a cast of thousands who used to hang around. Obront would have one lady on one side and another lady over on the other side. There was his chauffeur, Leo, who was in charge of getting Willie whatever he wanted. That impressed me. Who ever heard of a chauffeur? Another guy was in charge of cigars. It was the job of a guy named Dinky Levine to tell jokes. Joe Frankel was usually there. He was in charge of Obront's laundry business. He weighed about five hundred pounds. I think several years later somebody killed him.

For Gerry Pencer, this was the big time. I had a seat at the table. I wasn't doing anything wrong, but I thought I was a big man. A player. Willie would be smoking his cigar. I'd be smoking my Monte Cristo. Who was I to be smoking a Monte Cristo?

My father didn't approve of my association with Obront. Neither did my brother Bill. They said you sleep with dogs, you wake up with fleas. But I was a kid, and I clearly didn't measure the situation properly.

Besides, I was too busy opening restaurants. In six months we opened four Curly Joe's. Willie only had an interest in the first one. He never lent me any money. He put the money in the restaurant to do the renovation, and that was it. I changed the steak-house concept at Curly Joe's. I put in an open-hearth broiler in the middle of the restaurant, which gave a very nice feeling and the smell of the food. And I introduced a forty-five-item all-you-could-eat salad bar. On every table you had a fresh egg loaf and a pumpernickel loaf with a knife sticking out of it and a pot of butter. I got that idea from a restaurant I went to when I was a kid called the Pub at the Newport Hotel in Miami. You could get a choice twelve-ounce steak, with salad, bread, and some great apple pie for dessert for $3.95.

Our food costs were supposed to be about 35 to 38 per cent of our profits, but it generally ran about 52 to 54 per cent, which was high for a restaurant. But we had very low labour costs and high turnover. We opened up at 11:30 a.m. and stayed open until one in the morning and we were packed from the time we started. We sold a bit of booze but not that much. I was never much for selling booze. The margins on it were high, but it kept people at the table too long. So the idea was, sell them a beer, sell them a glass of wine, whatever, but get them out. If you were still at the table thirty minutes after you had finished eating, we took the ashtray off and literally threw you out. It wasn't a place to talk. I used to turn the tables seven, eight times a day.

I had all kinds of crazy promotions to get people into the restaurant. When the restaurant opened in the thirties, the price of a steak was 65 cents. So I had this crazy offer for guys who wore toupees: if they were willing to park it in the coat check, we'd feed him for the same price the restaurant charged forty years earlier.

We had a package that outclassed Joe's. We had better quality, better value, better service. Slowly over the next two years, we took away all their business. We had maybe 180 seats. They had maybe 400. In the beginning, they were doing ten times our volume. One day they had to close up, literally. We were greatly aided in our competition with Joe's by Johnny, my doorman. Whenever people were going into Joe's Steak House, he'd open the door and they didn't know where they were going and they walked into our place instead. I'm sure they enjoyed it a lot more.

I also owned the Bar-B-Q on La Ronde at Man and His World. I bought the Stagecoach Restaurant or, as it was known in French, La Diligence, in 1973. It was on the Decarie Strip at Jean Talon. That was a beautiful restaurant—a log cabin building across from the Blue Bonnets Raceway. It sat about three hundred people and had a beautiful lounge. There was a tremendous collection of Canadiana, with Tiffany lamps, old sleighs, and other things hanging from the ceiling.

Its former owners couldn't get the volumes up. So I took it

over and tripled the sales in about a year. I sold comfort food. If you ordered chicken, you got a whole chicken. I had a roast-beef wagon to carve the prime rib at your table. Prices were reasonable. There were also baby back ribs, chicken, prime rib, and dessert wagons with seventeen-inch-high whipped-cream cakes.

The place was usually packed. But there were days when you couldn't give the food away. So I came up with the idea to hold wedding receptions in our banquet rooms. Not real wedding receptions. There was no bride or groom or ceremony. We just had the party. I figured everybody loves to go to a wedding, with all the dancing and getting dressed up and food. So I used to run wedding receptions on Sunday night. We used to charge them $5, I think. People really used to enjoy themselves. When beer was $1, I used to sell it on certain days for 19 cents. So we had a lot of fun with that and turned it into a wonderful restaurant.

I used to sit at the bar, suggesting football plays to Marv Levy, who was then the head coach of the Montreal Alouettes, and one of our best regular customers. After that he went on to coach the Buffalo Bills. We had a great band, and there would always be bar clowns, plus a few hookers hanging around.

I had a cousin who surfaced from time to time at the Stagecoach. All of a sudden he was the new shooter in the bar, telling everyone that his cousin owned the place. He would make a beeline to some women at the bar who were of questionable background. One night he checked in with these two girls at their apartment, promising them thousands of dollars. They're cooking him filet mignon, and there's wine and Champagne. This goes on for about three days, and not only does he not have any money, but he sells them a watch for a couple of thousand dollars that wasn't real. Then he takes off and leaves me, the famous cousin and impresario of a thriving business, to sort the whole thing out.

I don't think Nancy quite understood the scene. She was a little naïve in those days. But she let me do the things that the kid in me wanted to do. I guess she knew that if she wanted to keep this thing together, she had to let me live my own life. It was tough on her getting started. Not many wives give their husbands very much freedom. The reason that this marriage was so successful is that I think like an artist, and I needed someone understanding enough to understand me—that I needed, in a way, to be free. She knew what kind of person I was, and she was able to accept that.

There were a lot of nights I came home late. The odd time I would have had a few drinks. Not enough to make me drunk, but a few. Now I don't drink at all. I think it's foolish. But in those days it was a macho thing to do. I was a tough guy when I was young. Nancy and I didn't fight a lot, but when we did we had beauties. I remember breaking a dinner dish. That was my favourite thing to do when I got mad. I'd take my dish and smash it down on the table and bust it because I was so frustrated.

My other business victory at the time was buying the restaurant Miss Montreal from a bunch of guys who couldn't make it go. By that time my former employer was long gone, so I didn't get the satisfaction of firing him. It was very tough to make a go of this place. We had something like eight hundred seats. I came up with a plan to divide it into two parts: half would serve Chinese food, and the other half would serve Jewish food. The Chinese side was called the Wong Number and was run by a guy called Roger Wong and his family. And then we hired the chefs from a very famous Jewish restaurant called Dora's.

The trouble was both sides had to share the same kitchen. One Sunday night when we had over a thousand people to feed, the Chinese chefs got into a fight with the Jewish chefs. And the bottom line was that all the Chinese people quit in the middle of dinner and the wonton soup started tasting like matzo-ball soup. Mitzi Dobrin, the president of Steinbergs, waited in line for her Chinese buffet that night, only to find out that the pineapple chicken tasted more like chopped liver.

The place couldn't pay its bills. I had about five or six partners, and one of them was in laundry. I remember going to a meeting where he complained about us getting rid of the linen tablecloths. The reality was we couldn't afford to pay for them. Rather than embarrassing him and not paying his bill, I thought it was better to switch to paper napkins. He didn't agree.

I was partners in that with Gerry Snyder, who, as a city councillor and the vice-chairman of the Montreal Executive Committee, was the most powerful English-speaking politician in town. He would go on to be on the 1976 Olympics organizing committee. Gerry was a great guy. He never got the recognition he deserved for bringing major league baseball to Montreal. A few years later he won a big libel case against the *Gazette*, which called him a representative of the "Jewish Mafia." Gerry's defence, which was brilliant, was that he was a practising Roman Catholic.

I bought the place from Leo Goldfarb, who was Sam Steinberg's son-in-law. He was president for a long time of the Bonaventure Plaza. Before that he ran Ivanhoe, which was the big real-estate subsidiary of Steinberg's. Leo's a real straight shooter.

Gerry Snyder and I also owned a few race horses with Gordon Callaghan, a photographer, and Keith Waples, a trainer.

I'm not a gambler, but I found the idea of owning horses intriguing. These horses all had names like Pentathlon and Triathlon. They raced at Blue Bonnets in Montreal and Greenwood in Toronto. Once one of my horses was in a big race, so I brought all my relatives to watch. I was really proud. Well, this horse might as well have been running backward. I was pretty embarrassed about it, but it's funny now.

I was on another trajectory. In 1971 I created Cartier Maintenance Services Ltd. as a subsidiary. It provided janitorial and all-purpose maintenance for our institutional and industrial clients. By 1973 I had seven Curly Joe's in all—in Sherbrooke, Quebec, Le Bazaar Shopping Centre in St. Laurent, and all over Montreal. When my son, Clarke, was born in 1973, I was opening a Curly Joe's in Place Vertu. I also had opened two gourmet takeout food stores called Epicure Shops. We had plans to open sixteen restaurants in Quebec and Ontario. The restaurant business is fun as long as they're going well. The success rate for a restaurant is probably one in four hundred. I had a whole bunch of successful ones, which makes me optimistic about fighting this bloody disease I have. But that's getting off topic.

One day in 1973 I opened the paper, and lo and behold there was a story that the Quebec Police Commission of Inquiry into Organized Crime was investigating Willie. That came as a big surprise to me, even though there was always talk about Willie. I was naïve, I guess. I heard that maybe he ate dinner with the infamous "Vic" Cotroni or something, but I didn't think about that. If anything, I thought it was fun. I didn't really understand what the Mafia was. I didn't understand that these guys ran the unions, ran everything. I saw them as these guys on TV, rushing around with machine guns, putting guys in the trunks of cars.

I figured Obront was just a fringe guy, a hanger-on. It was not as if he was hiding something. These people had big entourages, and he was one of them.

Robert Cooper was the prosecutor. He's now a senior Hollywood producer. He called hundreds of people *in camera* to talk to them about what they knew about Obront. This went on for years—between 1973 and 1976. I was one of them. I testified *in camera* in February 1974 and again in November 1976. I went by myself. They asked questions about my partnership with Willie—what we talked about, about our financial arrangements. Mr. Schneider, who owned the restaurant where we used to eat, was even called as a witness, which was the biggest joke of all time. He wouldn't have known a thing.

Willie certainly didn't want to talk a lot about his friends, so they kept throwing him in jail for contempt of court. It's actually pretty awful. You shouldn't be allowed to do that. The commission ended up saying that he was a banker for organized crime and that he was involved directly or through front men in something like forty businesses around town.

In 1979 he was convicted of tax fraud for underreporting income. Willie ended up moving to Florida in 1980 and became a U.S. citizen. Then a few years later he was convicted of trafficking in counterfeit Quaaludes and ended up with a twenty-year jail term for drug trafficking. A few years after that he was out of jail waiting for a retrial or something, and he was convicted of doing the same thing. He was brought down with Nick Cotroni, the son of Frank, who was famous in the Montreal underworld. What confuses me about Obront is what happened to him. I would have never ever dreamt that this guy would fall for some dope thing or something ten or twenty years after.

The whole thing was really uncomfortable for me. No one is

accusing me of doing anything wrong, but now I'm partners in two restaurants with this alleged Mafia captain. The closest brush I ever had with the law was when I was about twenty. I was driving my Corvette to a Passover dinner at the Steinbergs'. A police officer pulled me in front of the Orange Julep on Decarie Boulevard and arrested me for driving too fast. He clocked me in at ninety miles an hour. I was so scared. He put me in the back of the police car. My brother Sam came to bail me out. We found an excellent lawyer who convinced the judge that if the policeman was several hundred feet behind me, how was he able to note all these facts in such great detail.

While the crime commission was going on, I went to Willie and told him how uncomfortable it was for me. I explained that my father and brother were coming down hard on me and that I couldn't deal with the pressure. I said that either he had to buy out the interest in Curly Joe's from me or I'd buy out the interest from him in those restaurants. And he agreed and sold me his interests in the restaurants at a very fair price.

I also bought Obront's meat-packing plant, Salaison Alouette, which was essentially bankrupt, after Obront went to jail. I had to do something because, number one, he was a very important source of supply to us, and, number two, we were getting very good extended terms to pay for our product. We bought his business for $200,000. We figured it was cheaper for us to lay out $200,000 than to have to pay our bills because we would buy maybe $300,000 a month.

My partner, Sam Rubin, and I made a proposal to its creditors through Dan Kingstone, a lawyer. Sam was my accountant, and we had been partners since I started up the catering business. But he brought together a group of accountants to invest in the business.

We called it Gerbin Packers, for *Gerry* and Ru*bin*. And then we sold that business to this new company that was a partnership between myself and Arthur Child, the president of Burns Foods in Calgary, which was the biggest meat packer in the country. Child had a little company called IMB Meat Products in Edmonton, which was selling cuts like ribs and loins to the food-service industry. I sold Burns meat products in bulk to restaurant businesses and caterers.

Burns supplied Obront. I convinced Child to buy the other half of the meat-packing business. We worked out a deal which transferred ownership of the packing plant to a new company, Burns HRI Ltd., which was set up to provide meat to hotels, restaurants, and institutions. Burns Meats had 51 per cent and Gerbin Packers (1975) had 49 per cent.

But the news of the crime probe and my old partnership with Willie almost put the kibosh on the deal with Burns. Just when they were ready to sign, they caught wind of this dirt. I knew that the rumours and speculation could kill the deal, so I took the matter in hand. I hired a couple of actors as my references, posing as people associated with the commission to talk on telephone to Ron Jackson and John Neilson at Burns. They convinced them that we were nice guys. It was just like Rolls-Royce—I had no credibility. They gave me credibility. They gave me a sterling recommendation. That's what any cop associated with the probe would have told them if they had bothered to ask them about it. I just facilitated it.

We merged the companies, and then we operated the restaurants and the meat-packing operation. Irving Choran went in to run Gerbin. He was an old friend of mine. He and his wife, Anna, became good friends of Nancy and me and we had lots of fun times together. He's still in the business today, in Montreal.

As a matter of fact, his daughter Adrienne married my brother Bill's son, Gary.

Around that time I got the idea of moving to Calgary. There were a lot of reasons to leave Montreal. For one thing there was a bit of shame over the Obront affair. My family was on my back. I don't think my brother Bill let me forget about it for fifteen years. It was guilt by association. I thought that by moving you kind of get rid of that curse. I ran from this thing for twenty years.

Obront called me a year and a half or two years later, I forget from where, and I thought long and hard whether I should take the call and decided not to.

I don't know what would have motivated me to pick up and move to Calgary, which I knew nothing about. In those days a Jewish family in Montreal never moved anywhere. You stayed put. I needed a shock. I just wanted to shock myself. Maybe it had a lot to do with my internal radar for opportunity. Quebec was on the slow track. The Parti Québécois had just been elected (it was 1976) and Anglo offices were defecting to Toronto by the dozens. It seemed obvious to me that Quebec would be in turmoil, which is how things in fact played out. But Alberta was in the middle of an oil boom. Calgary was thriving. I had travelled there a dozen times on Burns business and liked what I saw.

It also didn't break my heart to wind down my relationship with Sam Rubin. It's not that he was a bad guy. He actually was pretty intelligent, but from time to time I found myself questioning what he was telling me. I haven't talked with him now for maybe twenty years, but I'm sure he hasn't changed.

I would be wrong, though, to say there was any big strategy at work here. My life in Montreal was pretty much about survival. I started off with the bubble-gum machines and ended up with a fully integrated restaurant, food service, then into meat packing. You might say, "It sounds like strategy to me," but that's how it happened. It was always an adventure. And it was time for another one.

Calgary

Moving to Calgary turned out to be one of the best decisions of my life, even though my relationship with Burns lasted about ten minutes. It was inevitable. They weren't used to doing business with entrepreneurs. And they certainly didn't have a clue about how to deal with me.

At Burns my office was at the stockyards, which is not the most aromatic place. Years later, when I was at Cott, I bought the same stockyards to build a soft-drink plant there. In the end, I found that we couldn't get the right zoning for it, so we sold the land again.

I was dealing with Arthur Child, Burns's president. And then with Ron Jackson, who bought the company. His twin brother, Don, is the guy who ran Laidlaw, the transport and waste-management company. Ron is a nice guy. I wasn't there for five minutes when I figured out a new way to add value to the product. Adding value is the most important thing you can do. It takes something that's a given and kicks it up a notch or two so it becomes special and desirable. And in the process, its value can go through the roof.

In those days, domestic loin of beef cost about $3 a pound, whereas loin from New Zealand, which was much better than the stuff from Australia, cost about $1.50. But though beef from Australia and New Zealand was really good, it was unacceptable to North Americans because the cattle were allowed to graze on grass. That changes the taste of the meat and makes the fat more yellow than white. But for North Americans importing the beef, it was never an issue because they sold most of it for hamburger or stewing beef or shipped it off to Japan. Or they sold it off to a steak house for a buck a pound. That was big business for Burns.

One night I woke up with a great idea. I figured that if you fed cattle in New Zealand a similar diet to that of North American cattle for at least four weeks before they were slaughtered, it would whiten the fat, give it more body, and make it comparable to domestic beef. Doing that would mean a slight increase in costs—instead of $1 a pound, it would be something like $1.25, but it would still be less than half the cost of the domestic beef and it would taste better.

In Canada in those days, once you reworked meat, you did not have to declare where it was from. So, for instance, if you went and took a whole cow from Australia and you cut it all up into little pieces, you did not have to say this is from Australia. You'd effectively reprocessed it. The next step was to bring this meat from Australia in cryovac, a plastic-packaging process for frozen food that takes all the air out. The meat ages in the bag for up to three or four months. If you took the bag off and trimmed the meat, and cut it into smaller pieces, it became domestic as well. Shipping added only a few cents a pound. I found a way of shipping it by air. There was such a discrepancy in value between Australian meat and domestic meat that I created a lot of added value. It had never been done before.

I talked to the people at Burns about it, but they had no interest. It was too wild an idea for a conventional meat packer. That's when I realized that these people didn't understand how to deal with an entrepreneur. Mr. Child was a very impatient man, and he was more interested at the time in fighting with his competitor.

A couple of guys I was working with at Burns left the company and started up business with me called Fortress Foods in February 1978. I was still working at Burns but resigned a few weeks later. I shopped the beef-laundering concept around. There was a lot of interest in western Canada from people at Woodward, the department store chain. Everyone in western Canada was interested. Before long, an argument ensued between me and Burns as to whose idea it was. Litigation followed. It wasn't exactly a secret that I started Fortress, but Child was angry. They got upset and they sued me.

I wound up Fortress that September. I settled the lawsuit with Burns for a couple of thousand. Burns bought our interest in HRI out for about $400,000. I'd say we were equally wrong. From their point of view, I wasn't the right partner for them. My problem was that I didn't have patience. I wanted to grow it too fast. They were on a twenty-year plan and I was on a two-year plan. When you have people with such different visions, you're bound to butt heads. But you've got to remember, I was barely thirty years old at the time.

Now it was time to go and build something else. I suddenly found myself with some choices to make. Where did I go from here? What kind of business was I capable of running? I knew we wanted to stay in Calgary. We loved it there. Nancy thrived, making friends and becoming active in the community. Our kids were still little. Stacey was in Grade 3 or 4. We bought a really nice house there in an area called Britannia.

People took us into their hearts quickly. Overnight it seemed we built important friendships we've kept to this day. Everyone's door was open. You just dropped in on people uninvited. It was a great family place. A big crime story on the radio in the morning would be hearing about the 7-Eleven being robbed of $350.

That's a lot different from three guys being found in a trunk, which was the typical crime story in Montreal.

The one thing I could never adjust to in Calgary was the food. That was a major shock to my system. You couldn't get a decent bagel. It was like a soggy roll with a hole in the middle. There was a Safeway store everybody called the "Jewish Safeway"; they'd have some specialty items but it was really bad. Twenty years later it's a little better, but not much. Even the steak was terrible. When I was in Montreal all people would talk about were how great the steaks were in Alberta. It didn't take long to figure out that they sent all the great steaks to Montreal. Just like nobody in Calgary knew the difference between a good smoked meat or a good pastrami sandwich. The other problem was that there was nowhere to eat. It was big news when Swiss Chalet, the chicken chain, opened there. Even worse was that there was nowhere to eat on Sundays. Only the Chinese places were open. The Chinese food there was excellent, although there was nothing that came close to Ruby Foo's in Montreal.

So I took matters into my own hands. I bought an industrial-strength Chinese wok stove, the kind they have in restaurants, for about $1,500. Then I discovered I couldn't install it without adding a fire wall. That cost another $2,000. Then there was the problem of installing a proper exhaust system and stainless steel surrounds. Once that had been added, we were told we needed a commercial gas line from the street to the house, which meant digging up the yard. So by the time it was all in place, it set me back about $50,000.

But that's not the end of it. About the same time I came down with gall-bladder trouble, and my doctor told me I wasn't allowed to eat Chinese food. When my family moved to Toronto in 1987, I took the whole thing with me. And we installed it all over again. I've probably used the thing twice. I could have flown twenty people for dinner in Beijing for less money. But that's the story of my life. I get an idea in my head and I don't give up on it, no matter how difficult it becomes.

Financial Trustco

I didn't have to look very far in my search for something new. This was the great Canadian oil boom, and I was in the middle of it. Calgary was opportunity central. Things were so buoyant that it seemed you couldn't do anything wrong. The real-estate market was explosive. People were moving left and right. Plus, there were a lot of people from the east who wanted to invest in western Canada.

I'll give you an example of how hot it was. The first house we lived in was a beautiful place on Coronation Drive that I bought in 1976 for just under $200,000. A year later there was a knock at the door. Standing there was Bernard Isautier and his wife. Isautier has been in the oil patch forever. In those days he was president of Aquitaine Co. They offered me 40 per cent more for my house than I'd paid for it. I sold it to them on the spot. I regretted doing that for a while. But we ended up moving into a less expensive house, and I pocketed the difference, which came in handy later on.

I enrolled in a course to get my mortgage broker's licence, which I never did get. But while I was studying, I formed a little company called Bow River Capital that invested in second mortgages. I shared a tiny little office with a broker named Mike Begley. It was located in a strip mall on 14th Street off 12th on top of a chicken restaurant called Brownie's Chicken. All you could smell all day was chicken frying.

Begley would come up with deals and I'd vet them. There was no shortage of investors. A lot of people wanted to get money out of Quebec. Dan Kingstone, my Montreal lawyer, who was well connected, lined up a bunch of investors—Colin Adair, a top stockbroker at Richardson Greenshields; Tom Birks, of Birks jewellers; and Victor Marshaal, a real-estate developer.

One day Begley and I had a little difference of opinion. It ended with Begley tossing my files into the hall. That's how I met Bill Tanner, who shared the next office. Bill heard the commotion and came into the hall. He told me he had an extra office if I wanted to park there.

Bill was one of the strangest hybrids I ever met—a Mormon cowboy. He was a smart guy, and very affable. He was a real jock, and he liked to wear cowboy boots. Bill liked any kind of sport— golf, race cars. He was a very handsome guy, even with the scar he had on his face from a bad burn as a child. Women always found Bill really attractive. But he never paid any attention to that kind of thing. He was very religious. In fact, he was a bishop in the church.

Bill was doing real-estate deals here and there, including some in Banff with Jack Singer, who now owns a movie studio in California. He also had an interest in a restaurant called the Moose Factory. One day he sat down with me and Larry Shapiro, and we talked about going into business together.

Larry was the first good friend I met in Calgary. He ran an outfit called United News Wholesalers Ltd., which was a family business that distributed magazines to retailers. Larry always jokes about the first time he saw me, driving my cream Rolls-Royce down McLeod Trail, which was the north–south commercial strip. It was the first time he'd seen a Rolls. Calgary had never seen anything like me before. I was wearing a big fur coat that I had bought in Montreal, which was totally inappropriate. "Look, there's a buffalo driving that car," Larry said when he first laid eyes on me. Before long, Nancy and I were great friends with him and his first wife, Rhoda.

Bill proposed that we buy a building called the South Hampton from the Baizie brothers, Neil and Les. Shapiro was ready to go in on it, but then he called a friend of his in Montreal to check me out. His friend said don't invest. The Obront mess had followed me out west. Larry came into my office to tell me. He was really upset about it. We both cried. I told him I had been unfairly criticized for having mob connections, which were totally exaggerated. In the end, I convinced him to invest. Today he'll tell you it was the smartest thing he ever did. That's how South Hampton Properties was formed. Dan Kingstone and Larry were on the sidelines. Dan was useful in bringing capital to the table.

Then Bill figured a way to kick-start things. He had an option to acquire control of a company called Turner Valley Holdings, which was the oldest listed company on the Alberta Stock Exchange. It went public in 1914 during Canada's first oil boom. Peter Longcroft and Ken Sands controlled it. Turner Valley was in bad shape. In 1980 it lost about $44,000 on sales of $21 million. It was also all over the map. It had Honda and BMW car dealerships, a light-equipment sales company, a leasing company, a firm that used laser technology to align pipelines, and real estate. And the company owned some of the original freehold oil and gas rights, even though they probably pumped their last barrel fifty years ago. I immediately saw a lot of potential in this mishmash. Number one, Turner Valley would give us a platform to create a public company with a couple of thousand shareholders. That would give us a shell. Then we'd raise money within the company.

In 1980 we took South Hampton Properties public through

a reverse takeover of Turner Valley. We paid $1.3 million for 85 per cent. Nancy's mother gave me a good part of her savings to invest, which was a real leap of faith. Nancy's father had died in 1975, and she had a little insurance money. Larry Shapiro gave me $75,000. I invested the profit from my house. I owned 22 per cent, Bill Tanner 11 per cent. There was no plan. With the shell we figured we could raise some additional capital. The original idea was to sell off the car business for a few hundred thousand dollars.

Then the biggest fluke of all time happened. As soon as we bought it, Honda was taking off in North America. Everyone wanted one. And we had the exclusive rights for southern Alberta. It was crazy. You could sell a Honda for up to 15 per cent above the sticker price because there were so few available. So suddenly it became a gold mine. We were selling about fifteen hundred of these cars a year, and suddenly a business that had made $200,000 a year was making millions of dollars.

We built a new dealership in the north side of Calgary and added exclusive franchises for Porsche-Audi, Mercedes-Benz, Ferrari, Subaru, and Rolls-Royce. We effectively handled all the exotic cars and the imports in southern Alberta. By 1981 we were the biggest foreign-car dealer in western Canada, with sales of about $37 million.

We redid the third floor of the South Hampton building, which was near the Chinook Shopping Centre at 58th Avenue near McLeod Trail. It was a three-storey building with cedar siding and a big atrium in the middle. While we were renovating, Bill Tanner would jump across the atrium, which was about four feet wide. We'd all take bets on how far he could go.

◆ ◆ ◆

I met Peter Pocklington around this time. Peter, I suppose, will go down in history as the guy who sold Wayne Gretzky from the Edmonton Oilers to the Los Angeles Kings. He's certainly one of the all-time characters in this country. He's always up. He also always comes across as if he's being really candid. I met him when we agreed to buy his Ford dealership, which was the largest Ford one in Edmonton.

The negotiations for that business were a real comedy. We did due diligence and found out that the portfolio included a Learjet with no engines and $700,000 or $800,000 liability on it. He also owned this big property in northeast Calgary with a sour gas well that not only contaminated the property but contaminated the adjacent properties. He didn't know about any of this. But the most interesting detail was when we came with the Bank of Nova Scotia to check out the cars. We discovered a large percentage of those cars were converted, which means that he had taken the money and never paid down the bank. He couldn't get the money that he needed to pay back for the cars that he had converted and the deal fell through. I saw Peter last year in Hawaii. He was busy pushing one of those big-stadium Pavarotti concerts.

Then we embarked on an acquisition that would redefine our business. In 1981 we bought Financial Trust Company from George Mann in Toronto for $3.8 million. The company was only three years old, with two branches, one in Toronto and one in Alberta. It had $32 million in assets but it was losing money. Coincidentally, Jim Leach, the president of Financial Trust, had worked with Bill Tanner's father at Commerce Capital Trust.

Leach was a young upstart M.B.A. and a bit of a mercurial guy. But Tanner knew him and how to deal with him. We paid $1 million down and the balance over term, which was unusual. Not many sellers would do a term deal on a trust company. But it gave us the impetus to expand.

I moved the head office to Calgary. I saw it as an opportunity to do not only conventional trust-company business but some merchant banking and real-estate lending. Trust companies don't have to follow as strict guidelines as the chartered banks, so if you're running one you can be more entrepreneurial and get better leverage. It provided us with seventeen times leverage compared with only three times leverage you could get with the traditional bank. That gave us the access to do more things. It made a lot of sense, and at the same time we could do the conventional financing as well. The way I see it, the whole purpose of a business is to grow. And if you can grow in a regulated business, all the better. The economy was good and we were surrounded with talented people.

The next year I bought three Alberta branches of Eaton/Bay Trust Co. for $20,000 by agreeing to keep all the employees. They had $90 million in deposits. Bill Tanner's dad came to work for us. From the beginning we aggressively recruited new customers. On the deposit side we marketed a fabulous tax shelter known in the business as a loan-back income-averaging annuity package. It worked like this. Say somebody made $100,000 on the stock market. We'd sell him a tax-free annuity for $100,000 and lend him about $92,000 with the annuity contract as collateral. That left the investor free to invest the money. We would keep 8 per cent to cover our fees and interest differential on what the client paid on the loan and what we paid him on the annuity.

We were the first on it. Then the next federal budget clamped down and we couldn't sell them any more. But even though we lost the fee potential we were able to carry the loans on the books for the next fifteen years. It sold like gangbusters. In the first quarter we owned it Financial Trust reported a profit of $188,000 versus a loss of $80,000 the year earlier. Within a year we doubled Turner Valley's revenue. The stock rose from 25 cents to $2.75.

Here I am finding one time when I could do nothing wrong. Then bang, we go out and land $100 million in loans to find out that the assistant deputy energy minister, Ed Clark, had put the brakes on the boom with his National Energy Program, which gave the government a retroactive 25 per cent interest in oil and gas developments in federally controlled areas. It discouraged private exploration. It took one of the greatest opportunity locations in North America and turned it into utter chaos. The Alberta economy was hit like a ton of bricks.

Meanwhile, we were diversifying all over the place. My brother Sam came to run King of the Sea, a fish-importing business. We imported frozen kippers from England, lobster tails from Cuba, caviar from Russia, scampi. Sam had worked for my dad at Cott Beverages for a few years in the 1960s, then decided to become a food broker. He handled products like Lestoil and Brach's candies. He also got Steinbergs into private-label products, like toilet paper, hand soap, and cookies, that were sold under the S label. When I was in Montreal, setting up my vending-machine business, he handled a line called Moishe's Cole Slaw. Something happened with the supplier and I'd spend weekends with him, stuffing bottles of cole slaw so that he could sell them to Steinbergs and Dominion. Then there was a stevedore strike, and he was left on the hook for a huge biscuit shipment that didn't arrive. That curtailed his career as a food broker. Then Sam had an idea to sell insurance in Florida, so he moved to Hollywood, north of Miami, with his wife, Judy, and his two children, Jeffrey and Naomi. The insurance idea didn't gel for him, so he opened a couple of restaurants there, but found that business too seasonal. So he got into selling wheelchairs and adjustable beds. And he'd be dragging these beds up to the fifteenth floor of these apartment buildings. In 1980, when things were heating up in Calgary, I said to him, "Why are you killing yourself? Come to Calgary." He moved and I bought him a house and gave him a job.

Turner Valley was turning into a holding company, not unlike Conrad Black's Argus, except that it owned its various subsidiaries outright. We bought oil and gas companies to shelter money from other divisions and use cash flow for exploration and development. In 1982 we bought Petrostar Petroleum, in a share exchange. The plan was to operate and develop its own exploration plays, but we ended up rolling them into a package that could be exchanged for stock.

There wasn't any great big plan. The closest thing to what we were doing was Allarco Developments, which was a conglomerate of hotels, car dealerships, petrochemical plants, and television stations created by Charles Allard, an Edmonton surgeon who was pretty reclusive. We also set up some commercial and residential real estate projects in Alberta, B.C., Arizona, and Texas. We figured our food services and car divisions could provide the cash flow for financial services. I brought in CJ Food Services, which owned Curly Joe's. Maisonneuve was in full force until I started cutting it back maybe four years after I moved to Calgary. I kept my interest in the restaurants for three or four years and sold the institutional side of the business to

Versa Food for a couple of million dollars. Some of the restaurants we made money on, some we lost money on, but overall the experience was really good and I learned a lot. It was a great, great chapter in my life.

We were becoming so diversified that I thought it was a good idea to put out a newsletter, *Turner Valley News*, for our employees so they could understand the operation. I've always spent a lot of time cultivating the loyalty of my employees. Without that you have nothing. By 1982 almost a hundred of my six hundred employees owned stock in the company.

◆　◆　◆

In 1982 I met the Blumes twins, Moe and Mark. They had a concept called Mark's Work Wearhouse, which was a big-format store selling work clothes. Mark used to be a senior guy at the Hudson's Bay department store and Moe was an accountant with Peat Marwick. They were identical twins. Each one was about six-foot-three, 280 pounds, and they both liked to smoke these forty-foot-long cigars. These guys made some good moves but were socially challenged, seriously socially challenged. If you wanted to know what they ate for lunch the day before, all you'd have to do was look at their ties.

Ted Medland, who was running Wood Gundy in those days, fell in love with them and raised $10 million to take the company public. They ended up opening about eighty Mark's Work Wearhouses. It was a big business. But that was later. When I met them, their business was heading for trouble. They wanted to expand, but they didn't have any more capital. I wanted to help them but didn't want to put cash in from our business. So we did some fancy paperwork. Financial Trust took out a debenture that was convertible into restricted voting shares. Then in May Mark's Work Wearhouse bought the automotive division of Turner Valley by issuing a couple of million restricted voting shares to Turner Valley. We ended up making millions and millions of dollars profit on that car business. We took back shares for 40 per cent of Work Wearhouse. They wanted to bump their volume up, and it would give them more critical mass, and it made a lot of sense for them. A year later I sold our shares to Manufacturers Life and ended up being able to monetize our position. We sold it for about $8 million. Almost overnight we made a lot of money that allowed us to go into real estate.

Tanner and I had seats on the Mark's board, so we ended up listening to this fighting across their boardroom. It was awful. I got along fine with Mark but had trouble with Moe. He was always trying to do work for us, putting together deals, and we didn't see eye to eye. I told Mark to get rid of Moe, and Mark didn't take too kindly to that. So we left the board. Years later, the twins had their own falling-out, and Mark forced Moe out of the company. Then, Mark's board kicked him out too. I hear the brothers don't talk to each other. I don't blame either one of them!

In the early 1980s the real-estate market soured, and we had to write down a lot of bad mortgages. By 1982 we needed to raise money. Trust companies weren't exactly favourites on Bay Street. Greymac and Lenny Rosenberg had gone belly-up earlier that year. In January 1983 the Ontario government seized some $2 billion in assets held by three trust companies. The day that story appeared our stock dropped 60 cents. That was major, considering it was trading at $5. It didn't help that I looked a bit like Lenny Rosenberg, or so everyone said. I never saw it myself.

In July 1983 we changed the company's name from Turner Valley to Financial Trustco Capital Ltd. The Bay Street brokerage Walwyn Stodgell Cochran Murray Ltd. raised us about $10 million. The shares were offered at $6.50 each. We were into everything. Financial Trustco handled mortgage placement, funding, and servicing for real estate projects, and managed the Mile Hi lodge in Banff. Revenues had grown more than 100 per cent in the past three years. We had nearly $270 million in assets and we were growing more than 200 per cent a year. Other trust companies were growing about 20 per cent a year. We started getting national press attention.

Having become too big for our first office, we brought a six-storey structure at Fourth and Centre in downtown Calgary. We kept two floors and leased the others. We put in a trust branch there and built really nice offices designed by Arthur Fishman in an art deco theme, with chrome and dark grey. I put my first bubble-gum machine from Montreal on my coffee table as a reminder of my early days—if it wasn't my first one, it was one just like it. In the reception area, we installed this huge folk art sculpture of Noah's Ark on Mount Ararat after the flood with all the little animals walking into it. It was huge. The only problem was that it was set up so the animals were walking the wrong way. I didn't know that until a journalist who came to interview me pointed it out.

It was an exciting time, even though we had less than $20 million in equity. I worked hard at thinking of the ideas that brought this business to the little guy. There was no way we could succeed just being a little trust company. We didn't have the kind of resources of a company like Montreal Trust. We would have to depend on outsmarting them by giving the customers different services than anybody else offered. We focused on service in the mortgage and deposit operations. We offered higher interest rates than the banks to draw customers and faster loan application approval. We guaranteed to turn around a mortgage application in twenty-four hours.

I had the idea that we could build this unique kind of financial-service business that nobody had ever built before in Canada. It would be like a financial supermarket with a full line of services for middle-class earners. I would develop software technology to be able to give independent advice to consumers rather than the biased advice that they would get from a financial-service company. We would offer tax advice and long-term financial planning. It was probably an idea ten years ahead of its time.

It took me thirteen years to build $1 million of net worth in Montreal. In Calgary it took only two years to build $20 million. Anything seemed possible. In 1984 John Toma, who had just been fired from his job as president of Dominion Stores, came to me about attempting a buyout from Conrad Black. Nothing came of it, though. I had no interest in supermarkets. In 1985 Bill Tanner and I and a group of like-minded lunatics tried to take over the Calgary Stampeders from the non-profit foundation that owned it. Don't ask me why. The deal cratered when the city wouldn't subsidize the rent on the stadium. Thank God! Our plan to bring Minor League pro basketball to Calgary mercifully met a similar fate.

◆ ◆ ◆

I adapted quickly to the western way of doing business—deals were finalized with a handshake. In Montreal, you needed six lawyers and an accountant to get anything done.

I collected a unique bunch of directors at Financial Trustco. Bill Henning was a very prominent, very patrician Edmonton lawyer; Doug Hunter was an oil man; Keith Hartley, a Wall Street investment banker. Steve Halperin handled the legal work on our deals. A lot of the people I had met out there were real cowboys but really nice people. Jim Palmer was the big man in the west for the federal Liberals and senior partner of Steve's firm. He was an early Financial Trustco director and provided a lot of introductions. He was the chancellor of the University of Calgary and is now the chairman of the Alberta telephone company, Telus. John Burns, another lawyer who was a real fixture out there, was a friend. So was Rob Peters, who ran Peters and Company, one of Calgary's most successful brokerage and underwriting businesses. I met Rob shortly before the takeover of Turner Valley was finalized. He told me in no uncertain terms he thought my plan to turn around a crummy car dealership was a pipe dream. To my delight, he became one of the original directors of Financial Trustco.

About 1982 Rob invited me for supper at his house to meet Joseph Granville, who ran an influential stock-market newsletter out of California. At the time Granville was making his greatest predictions and had everyone's ear. Rob's wife was taking a long time cooking Cornish game hens, so everybody was drinking without any food in their stomachs and getting pretty pissed. I'll never forget Joe Granville playing the piano, three-quarters drunk. Then we finally sat down at the table. Just before he tucked into his hen, Granville took out his false teeth and handed them over to his wife to store in her purse while he had his dinner. I'll never forget that moment. After dinner, I got him to phone my dad in Montreal. He was one of my dad's idols at the time. So he woke up my dad to tell him the market was going up 100 or 200 points in the next day or two. I don't think my dad ever got over it.

As the businesses kept evolving, I brought in guys who were a bit more mainstream. During the $10 million IPO with Walwyn I got to know Fraser Latta, a young underwriter. He had gone to the University of Western Ontario, and worked at a number of Bay Street firms. Fraser was a good, sensible, ambitious kind of guy who had some spark in his eyes.

He's preppy, WASP, the total opposite of me. But he had a logical mind, and an eye for detail, which I figured we'd need. I felt he was a good kind of guy to stand up to me. He's able to look at the negative in everything; I tend to be enthusiastic about things. But in business you need someone like that who can bring in the opposing point of view and yet be smart enough to understand the opportunity and go forward. In 1984 I hired him to run my operations in eastern Canada. He handled non-trust lending activities and corporate development. He became my confidant. When Fraser's first daughter, Jennifer, was born, he and his wife, Heather, asked Nancy and me to be her godparents.

I never hired people through headhunters—I've always met them and hired them. I hired Ken Winger from Trimac in 1984 to become the president of Financial Trustco. Winger was sort of a Caspar Milquetoast type, but he was a capable administrator and an honourable guy. Before Ken, I had recruited Bill Neapole, who ran the main Calgary branch of the Royal Bank, to head up our trust company. Bill then left us to become president of the ill-fated Northland Bank.

In early 1984 I brought in Norman Steinberg, a prominent Calgary developer, to head up Financial Trustco Properties. Norman was a tough, cantankerous guy. He was ten years older than me, but everybody said we looked like twins. We did okay, considering that the real-estate market was sick. We always thought more like a developer than a bank. We'd be involved in every stage—planning, leasing, selling the project.

◆ ◆ ◆

On October 3, 1983, my father died. He was seventy-one going on forty. He was healthy until he was sixty-nine. Then he was diagnosed with colon cancer and was sick for a year and a half. It metastasized to his liver and they couldn't even give him anything. I didn't deal with his illness very well. I couldn't handle the sight of him sick. Before my dad died, he wrote me a letter asking me to look after the family. His death left a big hole in my life. And quite frankly, that's never been filled.

But even at the end my dad was a joker. After my mom died, my dad remarried a woman named Alice Abelson, a widow he met through Mrs. Steinberg, my brother Bill's mother-in-law. After that everything shifted for him socially—whom he played cards with, even his golf club. He joined Elmridge, which was the fanciest Jewish golf club. Before that, he played at Hillsdale.

After my father died, my brothers and I had to decide what to do with Cott, his soft-drink company. Cott had been up and down. One year he'd make $100,000, the next year nothing. In 1970 the company began selling bottled water under the Carignan label. That year there was a recall of all cyclamates, the sugar substitute, which was a big blow for Cott's low-calorie segment. In 1976 he bought a soft-drink production plant and other assets of a company called Private Brands in Mississauga to serve the Southern Ontario market. About 1980 my dad had done a leveraged buyout with the Silver brothers, who still controlled the Canadian rights. He got a little bit of outside financing and found a way to buy 100 per cent of the shares. He was always very proud of that. About the same time he had tried unsuccessfully to sell the business to Canada Dry for $1 if they would take on the debt and leave him the property in Toronto and Montreal. He figured that he could sell the real estate and walk away from it all with a profit. But things continued to get worse. In 1983 Cott lost nearly $400,000. Profit margins were shrinking.

Sam, Bill, and I met in Montreal with our auditors, Coopers and Lybrand. One of them said, "Okay, guys, my recommendation is to liquidate. It's worthless." We didn't pay any attention. It was an emotional decision. We wanted his work to continue. We wanted a company for his grandchildren. If we were going to keep the company, we had to deal with the debt load. Bill secured financing to allow the company to continue. Without that it would have died. So Sam moved from Calgary to Toronto to try to increase sales in Ontario and Quebec.

A few months after that I decided I needed to lose some weight. So typically I did it big. I enrolled in the Pritikin program in Santa Monica, California, for four weeks in December. Nancy joined me for two weeks. I arrive there and it's a dump. I'd brought a suitcase full of cigars. I'm figuring I might not be able to eat anything, but at least I could smoke. After I was there maybe about six hours, I get a knock on my door, and one of the staff says, "Mr. Pencer, you'll have to leave this place if you continue smoking." Now, not only my food is taken away from me, but my cigars too. It was terrible. I'd get up in the morning and have a medical examination. Then there'd be exercise classes, which I always tried to dodge or cheat in. Then they'd serve this unappetizing food—three ounces of protein a week, grains and beans. It must have been the flatulence centre of America. But I stuck it out. I lost twenty-five pounds. For a while anyway.

I met some interesting people. Dr. Nathan Pritikin, for example. I think he killed himself later. I'd kill myself too if I had to eat beans every day. Elsa Peretti, the jewellery designer for Tiffany, was there to stop smoking. Every night she went out to smoke. Another was Gene Roddenberry, the creator of *Star Trek*. He was a very nice guy, a very quiet guy. He had a heart condition. I also met this kid Tony, who was a farmer from somewhere in middle America. He was really fat and couldn't afford to stay longer, so I paid for some extra time for him. When Nancy came we went to Las Vegas and took Tony along. I'll never forget this guy standing behind a slot machine with two hot dogs in his hand.

While I was there Gerry Schwartz and his wife, Heather Reisman, came to visit me. Gerry had just moved to Toronto from Winnipeg to set up Onex Capital Corp., the first leveraged-buyout operation in Canada. I met Schwartz in 1982 when he came to visit me with Izzy Asper, his partner at the time in CanWest Capital, a merchant-banking operation. My first impression of Schwartz was this enormous Afro. He had hair up to the ceiling. Izzy and Gerry had come to talk with me about investing a fair chunk of money in CanWest. It wasn't an exciting proposition to me because I felt the opportunity was limited. I also didn't think that their partnership was long for the world. As it turned out Gerry and Izzy split the next year.

After they broke up Schwartz came and talked with me about helping him to finance Onex. I had a lot of confidence in him and became a significant investor from the outset. Gerry had an M.B.A. from Harvard, but he also had street smarts. Gerry and I formed an excellent friendship that would last for some time. I was named to the Onex board and executive committee and was active in its business from day one.

It was the first time I really got a chance to talk to Heather, who had her own career. She had married Schwartz the year earlier. I had met her in Toronto in 1982 at her son's bar mitzvah. She was a management consultant, which was a bit ironic considering that she had never managed anything. But Heather was impressive. She presents very well. And she had some interesting ideas for Financial Trustco. She was big on technology. I ended up asking her to sit on the Financial Trustco board and on our audit committee. She also reintroduced me to Jon Deitcher, who grew up on Cedar Crescent with me. Deitcher was an old friend of Heather's from Montreal. He was a senior guy at Dominion Securities and very close to Brian Mulroney, who was the prime minister at the time. Deitcher called me to suggest Sam Wakim would be a good guy to sit on our board. Sam was a lawyer and old friend of Mulroney's. I always found him to be a very pleasant guy.

Another politician who ended up on our board was Senator Jack Austin, who was the deputy minister of energy, mines, and resources with the Trudeau government in the 1970s. Jack had a really sharp mind. He was secretary to Prime Minister Trudeau. Andy Sarlos suggested that we take him on as a director in 1984 after the Conservatives were voted in. Andy was probably the best-known investor in the country. I met him in Toronto in the early 1980s. Sam Belzberg introduced us. Sam was the biggest cowboy of all time. He was one of roughest guys to work with that I've met. But despite all the politicians around me, we never used any political influence or even tried to. That was never my style.

◆ ◆ ◆

Schwartz introduced me to Mike Milken at Drexel Burnham Lambert in 1984. Mike was famous by this time for using junk bonds, which are high-risk but high-potential corporate bonds, to underwrite leveraged buyouts, which is where the buyer puts up about 10 per cent cash and finances the rest with debt. I was looking to increase my capital base in the company and leverage off that. Gerry knew all those guys from his days working with Jerome Kohlberg, Henry Kravis, and George Roberts at Bear Stearns and Co. Those guys had done some of the original junk-bond deals.

We made an appointment to see Mike at his Beverly Hills office at 4:30 a.m. That's when he saw people—between three and five in the morning. He wanted to squeeze people in before the market opened in New York. I met him at his famous X-shaped desk. He was juggling several meetings at a time in different offices. Mike's a very affable guy. And totally unpretentious. He lived in the same little house that he had lived in for years. His first chance, he went home to his family. His only affectation was his toupee.

I told him about my business. One of the keys to Mike's success is that he knows how to listen. What I was selling him wasn't very attractive on the surface: a small trust company in the Alberta real-estate market at a time when American savings and loans were sinking under their mortgage portfolios. One of Drexel's corporate finance guys said, "I can lose money at home. Why should I go two thousand miles to lose it?" But Mike liked my presentation and the strength of my management. It took him ten minutes to decide that he'd finance us. At that time, interest rates were very high, around 16 per cent. A month and a half later we had the money. We went to him for $20 million and ultimately raised about $50 million U.S. at 15⅞ per cent. In 1985, he raised another $60 million at 13.95 per cent.

The best thing about Drexel Burnham money was that it came into the trust company as equity rather than debt. It was supported by debt. That allowed us to borrow twelve to thirteen times that from the public. The resulting leverage allowed me to finance a series of corporate buyouts. We had so much money that we had to find a use for it. And it forced the company to grow more quickly than would otherwise have happened.

After that, we'd subscribe to some of the deals Milken was doing with Kohlberg Kravis Roberts, Duracell batteries and Safeway. All the guys like us had extra cash hanging around so we could place our cash quickly. We made a lot of money because we were getting commitment fees of 1 per cent. So if we agreed to fund $20 million for Safeway, for example, we would get a cheque for $200,000. In most instances we were never called on to even fund because they had it placed in another branch so quickly.

After working with Mike on that deal, I met his brother, Lowell. They were partners. He looked after all their own money, their partnerships and their buildings, Lowell also had a toupee. He still has one, I think, but Mike has taken his off.

I really respected Mike and the Drexel Burnham people. I think that they created enormous capital. They made things possible for smart entrepreneurs. They had their excesses, but then you look at the kind of businesses that they helped to create—names like Safeway, Duracell batteries, American National Can, Revlon. The list goes on and on. Mike always did what he said he was going to do. He also introduced me to a lot of great people—Ted Turner; the Australian financier Alan Bond; the financier Ron Perelman, who now owns Revlon, among a dozen other companies. Suddenly you get an appointment for tomorrow with a whole slew of them. He used to hold these big conferences that I would attend. I was fortunate enough to be on the A-list invited to the so-called "Predators Ball" that they hosted each year at the Beverly Hills Hotel, though I'm sorry to say I never went to any of the famous parties they held in one of the bungalows.

I feel Mike got a bad deal with his securities-fraud conviction a few years ago. I believe that if you do something that's terribly wrong, you've got to pay the price. But I think he was singled out for the abuses of the entire system. I think Rudy Giuliani, who was a federal prosecutor at the time, was on a crusade to nail him. Looking at the cast of characters at that time, Ivan Boesky and those guys, I think their sins were greater. Boesky was an inside trader, Milken wasn't. Not to say he was an angel.

What people don't talk about is the great job he did in helping corporate America get waste out of business. These companies had management that was sitting there, who didn't own any stock, and who had all kinds of anti-takeover provisions that nobody can get near them. They were running a private club and had lousy returns for shareholders. Milken changed all that. He forced them to wake up. People point to the failures. They say one or two deals collapsed, maybe five. These guys did hundreds of deals, and most of them were successful.

Mike and Lowell also helped me set up a private holding company called Granite Street. The name came from the street in Manchester, New Hampshire, where the head office of Cott was located. Drexel floated a $35-million debenture issue. Granite Street held my shares of Financial Trustco Capital and Cott. I had other investors, including Bill Tanner, Gerry Schwartz, and Dan Casey, who ran Creson Corp., a real-estate company. Dan owned about 11 per cent. Mike and Lowell Milken owned 8 to 10 per cent. It let me go out and raise another $50 million in that company that I could use for investment purposes.

Mike's a guy who has done nothing but good things for me. He put together more than $100 million for prostate cancer, which he was diagnosed with when he was in prison. He and Lowell have paid $1 billion in fines, but they still have a couple of billion left and they look after it. Ted Turner just paid him $50 million to give him advice. The regulators complained about that, but Mike got it. He's proof that you can bounce back from massive failure.

I never saw junk bonds as high risk but as a leveraging opportunity. From my side junk bonds were a good source of financing. How else could I build an entrepreneurial merchant bank with someone else's money? Let's be realistic. Whose high risk was it? Theirs. It wasn't mine. I didn't take the high risk. They did. The investor took the risk, not me. I didn't have anything when I started, so what am I risking? People would say, "You're insane to pay 15 per cent interest." But if you look at the marginal cost of that money on the basis of leveraging seventeen to one, it was very low. I don't think people ever understood that. So that whole idea of Financial Trustco was a little better thought out than at stage one.

The stakes may have been higher, but it wasn't unlike my bold venture into Steinbergs cafeteria in Montreal. I didn't see that as high risk. I guess you could argue that I never had anything to risk except my reputation and what my family thought about me. That was my risk. I was looking for approval from my brother Bill all the time, so the risk was that he would laugh at me or put me down. That was something I was aware of constantly.

But it's also this roller coaster. It's getting in it and the exhilaration of getting up to the first hill and then suddenly having to career around the corner, not knowing where the next hill is, and there's so much happening and there's so much excitement out there. You really have the choice: do I want to sit in the station or do I want to take the risk of making this happen?

For my fortieth birthday in April 1985, Bill and his wife, JoAnn Tanner, Larry Shapiro, and his second wife, Baillie, and our friends Joe and Sondra Spier threw a big party for me. They sent out invitations that looked like a stock certificate. The message was more prophetic than we knew:

The King of Convertible Preferreds is turning 40 today
and we are having a merger, to chase the slump away
A friendly takeover at La Chaumière to negotiate food and drink
so market on your calendar in red Inc.

Come out and tell a humorous story about the King
and a gag memento of some sort please bring,
We know the company will not go bust
For you will not sell him short, we trust.

◆ ◆ ◆

I met Michael Ovitz, the superagent, in 1985. I'm even proud to say I helped him build the new headquarters for Creative Artists Agency, which was the most powerful talent agency in Hollywood. Here's what happened. Financial Trustco owned 12 per cent of a company called the Western Federal Savings and Loans, based in Marina del Rey in Southern California. It had over $1 billion in assets. We were the largest shareholder with about 9.9 per cent interest. One day Ovitz bought stock in the company. He held about 7 per cent.

Ovitz and I were both there for the same reason, to help these guys to avoid a hostile takeover. He called me when I was in Los Angeles. That was his heyday as the power broker. He had Stallone; he had everybody. I went to see him, and we had a good conversation about the business. It was around the time he wanted to build the headquarters for Creative Artists. Western Federal had a terrific property, a branch right where that gorgeous building is now. We helped him finance and build it through Western Federal. It's the curved building, a landmark in Los Angeles.

It was through Mike Ovitz that I met Henny Youngman. Mike arranged for Henny to perform at directors' meetings I held for Financial Trustco. He came back three times for our board of directors' meetings, which were great. One was in Florida, and Tanner dragged me and Larry Shapiro to a golf camp in Boca Raton. The pros got together to create a unique golf swing for me that accommodated my stomach. And I mastered it. We played and I beat Tanner. He wasn't very happy about that, having this fat kid from Montreal beat his butt.

Henny's a very funny guy, but the problem is you can't get rid of him. He must be lonely. He loved to tell me jokes about his wife, who had been dead for about ten years. "Gerry," he'd say, "my wife just came back from Bloomingdale's and she had an escalator with her. So I said, 'What are you doing with that?' And she said, 'You know I always buy anything that's marked down.'"

I had to go around for a whole day with him at the rodeo at the Calgary Stampede. He wasn't there for the money. He came because he wanted to come to Calgary and he wanted to strut around the Stampede in this big cowboy hat. Let me tell you, a day with him was enough. He's a character.

◆　◆　◆

The market was getting pretty tough. There were arrears in mortgage portfolios. In 1985, two Alberta banks crashed. But we were steaming ahead. We had fourteen branches across the country with $500 million in assets. We also had six oil companies we had acquired over the past four years—Petrostar Petroleum, Bonn Energy, Yvanex Development Ltd., Audax Oil and Gas, Calais Resources, and Westmont Resources. We had plans to package them as high-yield investments and sell to the public under Audax. Then in 1986 the price of oil collapsed. But we did some great deals. In 1985 I hired Lawrie Savage, a former director of the federal government's property and casualty insurance division, to head up our insurance division. He spotted an interesting little company to buy called Elite Insurance

Company. We bought it for $2.5 million and took it public in October 1986. We sold 20 per cent to the public for $20 million, which put a value on it of $60 million. Not a bad return on investment.

In 1985 I also spotted big opportunity in a company called Morgan Bancorp. The next year we turned it into Morgan Financial, which was just under Financial Trustco Capital in the corporate pecking order. Financial Trustco was unregulated. Morgan Financial became the holding company for all our financial-services operations—Financial Trust, Morgan Trust, Elite Insurance Management Ltd., and Westbury Life Insurance Co. In October 1986 we took Morgan Financial public and raised $30 million. Trustco retained 80 per cent of the interest in Morgan after selling the $30 million worth of shares. So we achieved major growth and diversification at zero net cost. That was an exceptional program for us. Not only did it put us into a more diverse operational structure, but at the same time it demonstrated that we were capable of buying an asset at a hell of a good price and then multiplying its value overnight.

Ken Winger took over running Morgan. The idea was to consolidate all the regulated Canadian financial services in one separate company. I was hoping to maintain Trustco's deal-making freedom while Winger coped with government policy, which seemed to be shifting every half hour.

About the time we took Morgan public, I decided to float a Cott IPO with Walwyn and First Marathon, another Toronto brokerage, under the Quebec Stock Savings Plan. It went public on the Montreal and Toronto Stock Exchanges at $7 and then fell to $3. At the time I didn't think Cott had a lot of value as a business, so I figured that raising $10 million would give the company some capital that we could do something else with later. It was a good time to raise some liquidity. That was all I knew: creating value by shifting paper around. That's when I became chairman of Cott, though it was little more than a title. I was too busy at Trustco to think of much else.

◆ ◆ ◆

By this time I realized Financial Trustco had to relocate its headquarters to Toronto. I was spending more and more time there. I knew I didn't have a choice but to grow out of this problem. In 1980 we had just under $17 million in assets. By the end of 1986, we had assets of almost $2 billion. We had a $100-million mortgage portfolio underpinned by weak real-estate values. I couldn't afford to just get all those mortgages off our books, so I had to work through piece by piece. One of the ways to do this was to continue to grow the company. If we went to Ontario we could double the size of the portfolio. Having another $300 million or $400 million of Ontario mortgages made a lot of sense at that time, and also it allowed us to diversify the portfolio much more in a province that had a lot more liquidity. The whole world was in Toronto. It was another road, another challenge.

Making the move was difficult for my family. They loved the life we had created for ourselves in Calgary. We had wonderful friends. There were Tammy and Noel Purkin (Noel was our family's physician). And Toba and Bill Friedman (Toba and Nancy were best friends). Nancy thrived. I bought horses for my kids. I even tried to ride myself. One of my dealerships, Lone Star, sponsored a chuckwagon in the Calgary Stampede chuckwagon race. In 1981, I rode it in the Stampede, though I left the racing for the pros. In the summers we went to Kelowna, British Columbia, and stayed in this little three-hun-

dred-square-foot cabin on the lake. We flew in lobsters for big
cookouts with a lot of our friends. We had a really great time.
We were famous for our dinner parties. I loved to cook. Once I
nearly burned a friend's kitchen down, flaming cherries jubilee,
just like when I was a kid.

We also became involved in the community. I was the Top
Gifts Chairman for the United Jewish Appeal's fundraising cam-
paign in Calgary and Western regional chairman for the Hebrew
University of Jerusalem. People would hide from me when I
approached them for a donation because they knew they could
never say no. I also did a lot of fundraising for the Calgary
Philharmonic Orchestra. Once we had a pie-throwing contest
for charity in our living room. Our house was done mostly in
white, so it was quite the spectacle. Noel Herschfeld, a prominent gastroenterologist in town, took one right in the face. I
even bought the Calgary Philharmonic for an evening at a charity auction so I could lead the orchestra. Another big auction
prize I bought was a dinner with Dr. Ruth Westheimer, the
famous sex therapist, at her house in New York. It included a
free consultation for a half dozen of my best friends. I paid the
$10,000 but I never went.

During our time in Calgary my son, Clarke, was very ill. Just as
I was starting up Financial Trustco, we discovered that he had
inflammatory bowel disease. He spent months at a time at
Rockyview Hospital, Alberta's Children's Hospital, and the
Foothills Hospital in Calgary. We went to doctors in Calgary,
then to the Mayo Clinic in Rochester, Minnesota. They all
talked about ulcerative colitis and Crohn's disease. His first

surgery, to insert an internal pouch to function like an ileostomy, was at the Mayo in 1984. His doctors in Calgary were angry because we opted for a more radical procedure than they had recommended. It was my first taste of medical politics.

In 1987 we consulted with Dr. Fonkalsrud, a top colo-rectal surgeon at UCLA. First, he said the internal pouch should be repaired. Then I put my foot down. I wanted the pouch out. I didn't have any hard medical data, but it just didn't make sense to me that Clarke had had something sitting in his gut for years. He had spent the previous year of his life in bed. It was as if he was being slowly poisoned. So they removed the pouch. That surgery saved Clarke's life. It was a miracle. There was an immediate change. He still had to have more surgeries, for obstructions. But then he became better. The whole experience was wrenching for the family, but it taught us that you can never give up hope. Often doctors don't have too much hope, but you can't let that influence you.

In late 1985, just before I moved to Toronto, I got into a beauty of a fight with a neighbour. It began when I wanted to build a basement apartment that we could use for a housekeeper for Clarke, who was still really sick. I actually had four houses in Calgary. The first was the one that I sold to Isautier. Then I moved to a second in an area called Pump Hill, and then we bought a bigger house. Then we bought an even bigger one in an area known as Eagle Ridge. But I wanted more space, so we decided to renovate. We got a permit from the city. We started with the basement. And, as is the story of my life, one things leads to another. Before you know it there's a bedroom and a new family room. Three floors later we had spent $255,000.

Our next-door neighbour's name was Arnold Churgin. He owned a bunch of shoe stores in Calgary. He was not happy with all the activity. He complained, which led us to the discovery that a clerk in the planning office had made a mistake. We lived in the only area of Calgary that insisted on a ten-foot side yard between houses rather than the standard eight feet. The rule said there had to be 2.4 metres on each side, but the addition took up half of that. So I had to remove four feet, which was the same as taking the whole thing down. It would cost me $100,000 to rebuild.

Ron Ghitter was my lawyer on the Churgin matter. He was a major presence in the Alberta Tories; he's a senator now. Ghitter had lined up a sweet deal to buy a resort hotel in Kananaskis County. It was Premier Getty's dream for an Alpine village at Ribbon Creek. We started construction of a second hotel next door, backed by a Revenue Canada promise of a tax write-off. We took it public, sold out the shares, and made about $5 million with fees. And during the time I was there I developed Kananaskis and built the hotel, with a few Canadian Pacific hotels, for the 1988 Winter Olympics.

Anyway, Churgin complained again to the city. The mayor at the time, Ralph Klein, who's now the premier of Alberta, I knew very well. So I called Ralph and I said, "What am I supposed to do, you gave us this permit from the city, now what am I going to do?" So Ralph said to me, "You know what—because we made a mistake, we'll rezone your house, but you'll have to make a new application for rezoning."

We got into an enormous fight with city hall over this. Half the people in our neighbourhood were on one side and the other half who were friends of mine were ours. I understood the position of the people against me. I now had this house with eight thousand square feet sitting next door to a house with twenty-five hundred square feet. They could look out their window and it kind of didn't really go together. It was a front-page story in *The Calgary Herald*. It polarized the entire community.

We won at the city and they rezoned my house. So Churgin decided to take me to the Supreme Court of Alberta. He argued that my house was rezoned in the private interest, not in the public interest. He accused Ralph and those guys of being nice to me. I lost. I received an order to rip my house down. But in the meantime I was planning to move to Toronto.

The bottom line of the whole thing is we won in the Court of Appeal. But by then Mr. Churgin had dropped dead of a heart attack. And we had already bought another house in Toronto. We left the house in Calgary empty for a year while I tried to sell it. Finally a guy by the name of Kwinter from Toronto, a lawyer, comes and buys the house. His father owned Kwinter's hot dogs. He wanted a survey done. When we did, we found out that not only did the city make a mistake on the plans, but we went over three inches when building on the property. The way I like to think of it, Mr. Churgin, in his final resting place, knows the house is three inches off side. And maybe he's planning on coming back for another big battle.

By the time I came to Toronto in 1986, we had built more credibility in the business. In October we opened a branch in Halifax, our sixteenth. We had more than fifty thousand customers. Fraser Latta was already there. Norman Steinberg came with me. Bill Tanner didn't want to move from Calgary, so he stayed there to run the real-estate business. My family followed me in June 1987 because we didn't want to disrupt the kids' schooling. Lawrence Bloomberg, the chairman of First Marathon, told me about a great house coming up for sale. We bought it on first sight. We were lucky; we got it for $2 million, which was a great price in that market. Then we hired Joe Brennan to gut it and renovate. The house is spectacular, done with Nancy's great style.

The new offices for Financial Trustco were on the twenty-fourth floor of the Standard Life building, smack in the middle of the financial district. I shared space with Andy Sarlos, who managed a lot of the company's money. Andy was considered some kind of oracle. The Buddha of Bay Street, somebody called him. He emigrated from Hungary and bought a company called HCI, a dormant fireworks factory, of all things, and ran profits through the roof. He cultivated an amazing network. He knew everyone. After that, he invested money for some of the richest people in Canada. I put money in the Sarlos & Zukerman Fund, which was a high-risk, speculative limited partnership. Andy ran it with his partner, Barry Zukerman, who I felt didn't get the credit Andy did. It was into everything—arbitrage, futures, options. Everybody had money in it.

I liked Andy. He died last year. He was a great talker, and he was great in cultivating relationships and setting up introductions. But investing in his fund probably wasn't the wisest thing for me to do because he was the biggest shooter around. In the beginning Andy was good, but I listened too much to him and I allowed the portfolio to become far too high risk for the type of business that we were in. There wasn't enough diversification. Andy was a gambler at heart. He would call me up to bet about what the market was going to open at the next day. He'd bet on anything. He was compulsive, the way some people are compulsive drinkers. But he pretended he was a manager. And a lot of people believed him.

My office had a big mahogany desk and the trappings of a big financial-services business. I was totally out of place there. I didn't really think of it at the time. But imagine me having a meeting with Hal Jackman, who was running National Trustco at the time. I was never one for networking. I always ate lunch at my desk, never went out. The big restaurant at the time was the 54th on the top of the Toronto-Dominion Centre. I hated that. Part of it was that I can be shy in new social situations. But more than that, I thought it was a waste of time.

There was a big difference between the business cultures of Calgary and Toronto. Calgary people are very approachable. They're risk-takers. They're much more entrepreneurial. And they'll give the little guy the time of day. That said, I never felt like an outsider in Toronto. I thought I was this great entrepreneur who could do anything. Toronto signalled the beginning of something that was a little more strategic, even though it still wasn't a defined thing. I still had a few cowboys in that business, whether it was Andy Sarlos or our real-estate group. I took a lot of pleasure in being different from the pack. My first big gesture in the Toronto scene occurred the night of May 12, 1987, at Sotheby's spring art auction. I bought a Krieghoff, a habitant fiddler painted in 1852. It was estimated to go at $70,000 to $90,000 in the catalogue, but I ended up paying $239,000 after some competitive bidding over the phone. I knew I was bidding against Ken Thomson, the billionaire newspaper baron, who owns *The Globe and Mail*. It was a record price paid for a Krieghoff at auction. I did it to make a statement, to show that I had arrived, to outbid Lord Ken.

My second big gesture occurred the next month when Financial Trustco took a 40 per cent stake in Walwyn Inc., which owned the brokerage Walwyn Stodgell Cochran Murray Ltd., for $37 million. It was Canada's fourteenth-largest investment house. I wanted Walwyn to create a national sales network for our financial products. We had bought a minority stake in NFBC Financial Services, which had broken away from Investors Group. That gave us a network in Quebec of four hundred people selling various financial products. Walwyn would give us almost five hundred people. It may have been small, but it had a big distribution system. I realized we had to aggressively chase depositors rather than wait for them to drop in to a Financial Trust branch or one of Morgan Trust's three branches. The whole point of building up the delivery systems was so we could access lower-cost deposits. The shift from lending money to chasing deposits was key to keeping up the growth. My plan was to provide cradle-to-grave financial services.

Andy Sarlos tried to discourage me from buying Walwyn. He felt that the market had topped. I didn't listen. But when I did buy it, he set up a lunch at the 54th to introduce me to Tim Miller. Miller ran a retail boutique for Wood Gundy called 42nd Street. He was legendary, the top retail stock salesman in Canada. He was the guy who really helped to make MacKenzie Financial mutual funds succeed in Canada. Miller was a great big bear of a guy who liked a drink. He didn't know much about managing a business, but he was a hell of a salesman—one of the best I've ever seen. He had a common touch, so he was great with the average guy. But when it came to being a salesman, nobody could touch me. I'm not a man of big words, but I could communicate with practically anybody. That's the key. So if it meant sitting with the minister of financial institutions or the chairman of the CDIC, I could communicate well with him. I knew how to connect as well with people in middle management. I'm equally comfortably dealing with a janitor or a CEO. I learned to adapt very fast because I understand what it takes to make people go. That's the *padrone* part of me, the guy who's the nurturer, the person who looks after everybody because that's how I want to be perceived.

I liked Tim and hired him away from Wood Gundy in August. I guess that was my third big gesture. My hat trick. I wanted him, sure, but I also wanted the attention. I also hired thirty-five Wood Gundy employees. I walked out with the crown jewels of their brokerage business, their best people, in one day. There had never been a raid like that in Toronto. People aren't that smart. People go out and pay a fortune for a company. We bought it for nothing, without the walls. I bought half of the value of Wood Gundy but paid no goodwill for it. I had a complete infrastructure. Two minutes after I did that Wood Gundy launched a $355-million lawsuit. Miller was sued for $46 million. Eventually it all went away.

What appealed to the guys I hired from Wood Gundy was the fact we created a situation for them to be partners. Everybody feels that they own people. You don't own anybody. Loyalty counts for a fraction, but if you work for twenty years it does not entitle you to more than your franchise value. I offered key people incentive. Six people shared 10 per cent ownership in the new company. And each $500,000 in commissions earned a right to buy twenty thousand shares. Walwyn shares were trading at $8 each.

The brokerage was on a roll; profits were doubling. By mid-1987 Trustco had $120 million in equity and $2 billion in assets. Things were looking up. Financial Trustco was one of the top ten trust organizations in Canada. There were plans in the works to enter the American market by setting up a wholesale mortgage banking business in Baltimore. We had about ninety branches and 600,000 clients. But we had a hell of a lot of debt. We had almost $157 million worth of junk bonds on our books with rates between 15 and 16 per cent. But I wasn't too worried about it.

Then came Black Monday, October 19, 1987.

It all started with the market down two hundred points. It didn't seem major. Then it just kept on dropping. I was in my office with Bill Tanner, who was in town. We kept punching in the Financial Trustco stock symbol in the Quotron on my desk. By noon the stock was in free fall. Six months earlier it had hit a high of $21.37. Now it was around $5. We were in disbelief. I peed my pants. Or if I didn't, I should have. I had twenty lines going at one time. I was talking to Sarlos, talking to brokers. We were all commiserating. At the end of the day Financial Trustco shares were at $8. They had opened at $16.

Things seemed bad, but we didn't have a clue about the implications of the damage until later. All of us in the financial business effectively went bust that day. Walwyn lost I can't even remember how much market value, but it was huge. Granite Street lost a bundle. When the market crashed, a large percentage of equity was wiped out. My mistake was leaving Trustco's money in the Sarlos & Zukerman fund after Barry died of cancer in January 1987. He was only forty-five. It was tragic. I didn't realize we were so vulnerable. It took the stock-market crash to wake me up.

The problem was that the holding company didn't have access to cash unless it could raise or come up with it. It had about $40 million in cash requirements. Regulators insisted that the equity in Financial Trustco be replaced, but the only source of new equity was selling out private investments in the parent company, which was high-yield debt and very illiquid. There was a real flight to quality in the market, so we weren't going to get any value selling out a high-yield bond, a non-listed piece of paper. The real issue was how to get cash flow in the parent to pay operating costs and the ability of the parent to service debt.

In final three months of 1987, Walwyn lost nearly $5 million. Walwyn was dragging us down the most, but Morgan Trust and Westbury Life were also losing money. The Canada Deposit Insurance Corporation and the Ontario Ministry of Financial Institutions demanded that Financial Trustco raise more capital. The holding company may have been unregulated, but all the subsidiaries were government regulated. In the spring of 1988, we managed to funnel in $30 million.

But even in the middle of it. I was named one of the top executives of the year by *The Financial Post*. I came in at number six. Schwartz was number five and Garth Drabinsky, who was running Cineplex Odeon, was number seven. I was able to keep up appearances. The next spring, Tim Miller decided he wanted to quit smoking, so he bought two popcorn machines for the trading floor. One paper reported some story that I raked him over the coals for giving an $800 bill for them to accounting. The truth of it was that I wouldn't have cared about something like that. He could have bought one of those machines they have at Cineplex movie theatres if he wanted to. But the story was well timed. It made me look frugal. A few years later Miller died of a heart attack. He was only forty-three years old.

In April 1988 I created a furor in the Ontario legislature when I hired Don Reid as the chief operating officer of Morgan Trust. Don had been director in the loan and trust corporations branch of the Ontario government's Ministry of Consumer and Commercial Relations. Some guys in the government went nuts, saying that Reid knew about competitors' practices.

That summer Morgan Financial went out to raise $100 million through high-yield debt. We planned to use $20 million to pay off the debt in Financial Trustco Capital, but the market wasn't there and the deal was pulled. It became obvious we needed a hands-on manager. Andy Sarlos suggested I hire Ed Clark, a senior executive with Merrill Lynch Canada. Ed had also been a rising star in the Trudeau government. In fact, I didn't figure out until much later that he had been the architect behind the National Energy Program, which had screwed up our real-estate portfolios in the early days. And here I was paying him a lot of money to help me figure out what to do. I resented Ed when he came in. He was this real establishment guy. He and I were like chalk and cheese. But I needed to see if there was a way that we could resuscitate the business. I needed someone to help me to assess whether there were any opportunities, not that I thought there were a whole bunch. I turned over the chairmanship and chief executive mantle to him in August 1988. I stepped down from the board not long after. Ed brought in John Pelton, a guy he worked with at Merrill. Pelton became chief operating officer.

Ed was quick on the trigger and made some big decisions very fast. Whether a decision is right or wrong, he was prepared to make it without a lot of consultation. Of course there was a sense of urgency, but he was good at exacerbating that. He made his determination in two weeks: the company couldn't survive. Once the decision was made, it was an issue between the regulators and the company as to what we were going to do. That's when Andy Sarlos entered the scene again. He pushed us together with Peter Cole, the chairman of Central Capital, and Tom Hodgson, the president. Cole was a real character, known for his love of a good party. When Cole and Hodgson bought the trust company, my impression was they were not particularily concerned about the quality of the assets. They were just hungry for another acquisition.

The other thing about Ed Clark is that he proved to be an excellent negotiator. He's Mr. Smooth. He should go down as one of the best bullshitters of all time. He had Cole convinced that if he bought Financial Trustco, they would have the next Royal Trust. He had the regulators on his side, knowing that you needed to find some kind of solution. Clark got an exceptional price from them. It's probably what ultimately put Central Capital into bankruptcy.

There was a lot of hand holding that went on. The Ontario, Quebec, and federal governments coughed up $84 million in loan guarantees. Cole was nervous about the real-estate holdings, so Clark bought them back. But he kept Morgan Financial, which was the most solvent part of the business. Just as everything was about to be signed, we caught wind of a critical article about me that was going to run in *The Financial Post*. It dredged up all sorts of allegations about my past, including the fact that I knew Obront. The editors at the *Post* agreed to hold the article for a few days to allow the sale of Financial Trust to go through. The government was afraid there would be a run on deposits if it was printed.

This was my worst nightmare. Here I have an undercapitalized trust company and I'm about to get a story asking, "Would you trust this man who was partner in a restaurant business with this questionable character over ten years ago?" It was something I always dreaded. Whether I was in Burns Foods or I was in the trust business, I was always paranoid that somebody was writing a story about me and Obront. Finally this guy named Philip Mathias did it. I really value what others think of me. And I finally felt I was rebuilding credibility. Then I had to read this ridiculous story that made me sound like the star witness of the crime commission. I was never even called before it publicly. I was devastated.

Sure, I knew Obront. I bought meat from him, but so did a hundred other people. The writer took the fact that I owned one restaurant with him, the fact that he put up the money to improve it, and whipped it into his own concoction. By innuendo I was in the Mafia too. And I was about as far away from this Mafia as you are, or at least most of you are. But in all the articles, no one ever had anything bad to say about me or even be able to accuse me of any wrongdoing, any relationship with any of these people. I feel the press really treated me unfairly. On the other hand, as my dad said, if you sleep with dogs, you wake up with fleas. But this was as if I slept with fleas and woke up with pit bulls. These were pretty big fleas I had to scratch for a long time.

The bottom line is that Financial Trustco became impaired for two major reasons. One is that I bought a large stock-brokerage firm ninety days before the market crashed, and the firm was exposed primarily to retail business. A business that I paid $80 million for was worth $20 million four months later. Our position was simple. We used it as a merchant bank. We didn't have enough time to get into real trouble, but we were at the end of a cycle. Not all our loans were great, we had a degree of bad loans, but that's not what got us into trouble. The second reason we became vulnerable was that the company was undercapitalized for what we were trying to do. And it was the first one to get hit by the CDIC because it was the easiest to collect assets from. At least that's what I believe. A lot of the other guys were basically frauds. I got really pissed off being lumped with them.

◆　◆　◆

The late summer and fall of 1988 was a bad time for me. An all-time low. Ed Clark was working on my severance from the company. I had an office in my house, but I felt I should be going somewhere every day. But I had nowhere to go, and I was embarrassed by that. Nancy and I talked a lot about how I felt about a lot of things but she always felt I would succeed, that I'd bounce back and do something else. But after a while, when I didn't bounce back, my family became very worried about me. There was nothing they could do.

I thought about what I would have done differently. I thought if we hadn't bought Walwyn, the company would probably have survived. I spent a lot of time thinking about what I could do next. I didn't have a lot of options. It was also difficult to look ahead because there was still so much uncompleted business with Financial Trustco. I thought about going back to Calgary, but I knew it would never be the same. You can't go backward. I think that the one thing that takes me through everything is that I only look ahead. I don't look back. Gerry Schwartz offered me a job with him. But I was an entrepreneur. I needed to be my own man. I was thinking of crazy ideas, things just to occupy my time. I thought that there were so many financial transactions going on Wall Street that I could go in and run one of these companies. But I realized that would mean working for someone else. I could never be happy doing that.

I even considered opening an art gallery. I figured I had enough inventory from my own collection to keep myself busy. I had a fabulous Riopelle that I bought for $130,000 from the Mira Godard Gallery and sold a year and a half later for almost $600,000. I especially love his works from 1949 to about 1953. He was at his best. And I had a nice Varley portrait that I was really proud of. I bought Peter Pocklington's art collection and turned around and sold most of it. It included a bunch of Emily Carrs and a beautiful Lawren Harris. I made about $750,000 on that. I sold that to Schwartz, and he turned around and sold it again. I even went out and got some opinions from people in the business. Av Isaacs, who ran the Isaacs Gallery in Toronto at that time, and Peter Ohler, who probably has the best taste when it comes to Group of Seven work in Canada. He owned an art gallery in Calgary called Master's Gallery.

I never think about money. It's lack of money you think about. I was on the hook for millions. I owned 49 per cent of Financial Trustco. I was facing personal bankruptcy. I owed a huge amount in back taxes. Everyone was advising me to become more liquid. I had the house and a few million dollars in art. My Financial Trustco shares were worthless. I also had a little interest in Cott, but it wasn't worth much. I had no cash flow, so I was worried. The most obvious thing was to sell the house. I couldn't afford it. But I couldn't sell it. I had worked hard to build the house. But there was something more. It was a last vestige of my own pride. Losing it would be the last point of taking me apart.

Instead I sold much of my art collection. I sold Ken

Thomson some fantastic things—a Franklin Carmichael, and two Krieghoffs, including an interior of a sugar shack. It was magnificent. The Carmichael had stayed in South Africa for most of its life. It was shown at Wembley. Some guy bought it for £6 in the 1930s, and it stayed in that family. Then when these people died, they sent it to Sotheby's in Canada. The thing had been pretty abused. It was sitting on top of a fireplace for maybe forty years and needed to be restored. I bought it for $280,000 without knowing if it could be restored. We sent it to the restorer and it was gorgeous. I cried when I sold it. It used to hang over my fireplace. All those paintings meant a lot to me. When things went really bad, I spent hours and hours looking at them. I kept a few things, but I was upset at having to sell these masterpieces that I had worked hard to collect. I made about $2.5 million and lived on the proceeds for about two years.

When I left Financial Trustco, I was very well treated, as were the other executives. I believe that Ed Clark played a role in making sure that happened. He also negotiated on my behalf with the Edper Group, a huge conglomerate controlled by Peter and Edward Bronfman, to sell them the shares that I owned in Financial Trustco, which they bought as a tax loss because they were otherwise worthless. At first Ed didn't appear to be my friend, but in the end he was.

The guys who worked with me at Trustco landed in different ways. Danny Kingstone sold his shares and made a lot of money. He eventually moved to Israel. Larry Shapiro's stake in the company was worth about $23 million on paper at one time, but out of loyalty he didn't cash out on the way down. He jokes today that the four Financial Trustco sweatshirts he owns, which were all that he got out the company, cost him $23 million. He says,

"We had fun on the way up and we had fun on the way down." Larry's son Danny worked with a stockbrokerage for a while, then moved into Financial Trustco when it was winding down. He learned a lot about managing lawyers. A few years later he would run our western bottling operation for Cott before going into his family's business.

Jack Austin held a big stake, which he also refused to sell. He ended up investing in Cott a few years later and made forty times his investment. Bill Tanner didn't do as well. In June 1988 Bill quit as vice-chairman to return to his real-estate development company. He was getting bored. He was concerned that the company was attracting a bureaucracy. Bill was a risk-taker. He had his money tied up in Granite Street, which took a big hit. He had to file for personal bankruptcy in 1990. The most difficult thing was that he held stock in Cott at the time that he had to cash in. If he had held it, it would have been worth millions.

My banks helped me through a tough time. People were generally very supportive. Gerry Schwartz and Heather Reisman, and all my friends from Calgary, were there for me. Even my old friend Andy Sarlos was, though he got me into half of that debt. But I know I can never blame anyone other than myself. If you're the chief executive, the buck has to stop with you.

Now you might say that we didn't pay off all our junk bonds that I floated at Financial Trustco, the parent-company level, but that had nothing to do with depositors. The banks were paid back. The CDIC didn't pay out a cent. Obviously our shareholders didn't do well. Neither did bondholders in the U.S., but most of them were in Chapter 11 anyway.

◆ ◆ ◆

In the depth of my depression over the business and what I was going to do next, Danny Silver came into my life. Danny is a great psychiatrist and a great guy. He was at Mount Sinai at the time, and visiting him became the first stop of the morning. At that time Danny was the village shrink for a bunch of high-profile guys in the investment and business community. I'd give you a list, but who needs the aggravation it would bring. I will tell you, though, that one of them—someone who suffered a big-time insolvency a few years later—used to come out of Danny's office sobbing like a baby.

I really liked Danny but hated his office. I bought him all new furniture because I couldn't stand the junk he had. Early on Danny put me on Prozac, which I think is great. It ended my depression. I had great difficulty getting off Prozac. I tried a few times and then just gave up on the idea.

By this time my brother Sam was asking me to come to work at Cott. For months he'd show up at my door. Things were looking better. Sales had doubled in a year. He took me to the plant on Lakeshore Boulevard. "I've taken this company through the first stage," he said, "but with your financial smarts we can do wonders. Just think of it, Gerry." I could feel something—the tug of potential, maybe—but I was still so dragged down.

It was Danny who finally convinced me. He had heard all the other schemes I was floating, and he thought Cott made the most sense. He convinced me that building widgets isn't so bad, that it was a going-back-to-roots kind of business. It would give me more time for my family, allow me to live more conventionally than I had in the past. It took him months, plus a lot of Prozac. Of course, things didn't turn out that way. I didn't know that then though. I just know I was ready for my next life. I didn't know it would be the biggest ride of all. Until now, that is.

I don't think of mistakes the way other people do. In my life mistakes have always taken me someplace new. But I know now they were just building blocks. Everything has turned out fantastically because that gave me an opportunity that I otherwise would have never had.

Cott

G oing to Cott in the fall of 1988 was the best thing that could have happened to me. Where else would I have found a situation where I could express myself as well and build something as quickly as I did? But I didn't know it then. I didn't want to go to Cott. I felt it was beneath me. Here was this tiny down-market pop company that had no reason for being, with two little factories, antiquated both of them, and no management team. In those days, private label was an in-and-out business—cheap label, cheap pricing, cheap cans. You're in and you're out. No one in the industry took it seriously.

What could I possibly do there? I wasn't an engineer who could figure out how to build new manufacturing systems. My talent was seizing the opportunities nobody else could see. But with Cott it wasn't apparent how I could do that. Not in the beginning, anyway. Besides, Cott was my father's company, not mine. It was where my brother Sam had worked for the past four or so years. What am I going to do now? I asked myself. Create another mess? And this time I've got my family involved. I've got my brothers involved. They're shareholders.

I went to Cott to help Sam—or at least that's how I convinced myself. Maybe that's the dad in me, but for the past ten years I'd been looking after him and had this real sense of responsibility to make sure he'd be okay. The company was making a few hundred thousand bucks a year. Sam had been doing a good job in the years after my dad died. He had opened the big accounts—A&P was the first. He did a private label for them called Chateau. He also serviced accounts with Loblaw. We also sold the Cott-label cola at IGA and Oshawa Group.

Sam was very well liked in the trade. But being well liked and running a business properly are two different things. Sam doesn't understand where to get on and to get off. Or how to build relationships. He would disappear into his office for six weeks at a time, but you can't do that. You've always got to have your foot on that accelerator. My brother Bill was another story. I don't know if I'm right or wrong about this, but I never felt that he had confidence in me to run the business. I felt he knew that I could build the business, but I was never sure whether he trusted me from the point of view of looking after his inheritance from our dad. Not that he needed the money. He's done extremely well as a real estate developer in Quebec. But he's a cautious guy. He has a totally different style from mine.

When I joined Cott I went and borrowed every cent I could from the Royal Bank. I figured that if I'm going to do this, I'd do it better than it was being done before. I needed a big enough interest to motivate me. So I went and bought three times the shares that I had on the open market. I ended up with about fourteen million shares, while my brothers owned about three million each. They were trading for less than a quarter when I started buying.

Financial Trustco taught me a couple of things. One, you can't leverage the crap out of a business. When I took over Cott I decided that the balance sheet is not something I'm ever going to worry about again. I'm proud to say that in the nine years I've been at Cott, the company kept a very, very conservative balance sheet with tiny debt relative to its capital and its equity and its cash position. The second thing it taught me was that you shouldn't grow in directions that you don't understand, though for me that one is harder to adhere to.

In those days Cott was run out of Montreal. The day-to-day was handled by a guy called Maurice Chouinard out of the main plant in suburban Laval. He was the chief executive brought in after my dad died. He and Sam changed the way the company was operating. They eliminated store-to-store delivery and got rid of the trucks, which saved a lot of money. The price of six bottles of pop was reduced from $2.49 to $0.99 cents. The problem was that Chouinard couldn't get along with Sam at all. It was a real Frick and Frack situation. Going in to sort it all out was a little depressing, let me tell you. In fact, the only time I ever felt that I was going to work was when I went to Cott. Before that, I never thought of work as work. It was always what I wanted to do.

I think I've blurred a lot of the details of the first year. I hired Fraser Latta as a consultant. He had just finished helping wind down Financial Trustco. For a while, we worked out of my house or a tiny plant we had on Dufferin Street in Toronto. I knew there were certain elements we needed to have a real business. We needed a real factory. We needed a growing customer base. We needed a great product. We had none of them.

One of our first big breaks came when the Pepsi 7UP Plant on Viscount Road in Mississauga came up for sale. They were building a bigger plant. That's an interesting story. It could be a book in itself. The company was called Pepsi Cola 7UP Toronto, but it bottled for 7UP, Pepsi, and Orange Crush franchises in Ontario and expanded to buy a bunch of bottlers. Then in 1987 a group of employees got together to do a leveraged buyout with some assistance from the Bank of Nova Scotia. Their lawyer was a guy called Tom Baker and they also had a private investor named Michael Graye. It was a big deal. A few weeks later, the president, a guy named Fred Rosbrook, who had been part of the LBO (leveraged-buyout operation), died of lung cancer. So Baker, the lawyer, took over as president of Pepsi 7UP Toronto. None of the other guys had the ability to keep this thing going, but nobody liked the way Baker was running the business, so they staged a palace coup and ousted him. They locked him out of his office. The whole thing ended up in court. While it was in court, I convinced them to sell us this building and all their equipment for basically the cost of the real estate. I negotiated the deal with Russ Plawiuk, who was the head of operations for the company, on a handshake in May 1989.

This was a major stroke of luck for us. These were probably the dumbest people I could ever find. I'm not talking specifically about the people I negotiated with. In fact Russ was really smart. I ended up hiring him later. It was just the idea of it—of anyone who would sell something like this with millions and millions of dollars of infrastructure to someone who's going to compete with them. Of course they didn't see it that way. To them, we were just a nothing soft-drink bottler that posed no threat.

The next month the management group lost the lawsuit, so they were all out of work. That's where I found some of my best people. I hired Plawiuk and Paul Henderson, as the chief financial officer. A bit later I hired Mark Benadiba, the head of sales and marketing. Mark was born in Tangier. He's a real street guy like me. His family was very poor. He drove a Coca-Cola truck while he was in high school and university and has been in the soft-drink business ever since.

Then we started doing deals. That got me going. I bought a little private-label pop company called Tricopack, which was our prime competitor in Southern Ontario. Then we acquired control of Sun Mountain Beverages in Calgary. Tricopack had a little plant on Lakeshore Boulevard in Toronto and another one in Concord, Ontario, where we set up the corporate offices. It was an hour drive to Concord. My office was eight feet by ten feet. The closets in my house are nicer than that office was. The filing cabinets were empty. The floor was covered with cheap linoleum. That or mildewed carpet. I tried not to look at it. It was a real comedown from my office at Financial Trustco. There, I had the top floor of the Standard Life building. I still had the mahogany desk from Financial Trustco that Ed Clark was nice enough to let me keep, but it would have filled this entire office. I sat at an Arborite desk, on a cheap folding bridge chair. On the other side of the desk there was another bridge chair for visitors, not that there ever were any. Oh, I almost forgot, there was a window—looking into the warehouse where the cans were rolling down the assembly belt. Just getting into the car in the morning was difficult. Then a good deli opened in Concord called the Centre Street Delicatessen. That's when things started looking up.

We were still surveying our options. Plawiuk was analyzing our operations in Montreal. By this time Chouinard had left. He liked running the show and he finally figured out I was in the driver's seat. We called in independent advisers, and they told us to invest or to liquidate. We were always worried about spending. We still didn't have any guaranteed volumes for the plant.

In the fall of 1989 we moved into the Viscount Road plant. We did some refurbishing and bought new equipment from Pepsi. We also hired a half-dozen people from Pepsi manufacturing. Cott's first boardroom had pink-striped chairs and an old dining-room table from my house.

We basically had a plant that was ready to roll. It gave us capacity of fifteen million cases annually. That was the good news.

The bad news was that we only had three million cases of business. I figured I'd worry about that later. If I had sat around worrying where I was going to get our sales from, I never would have gotten the plant. I would have been thinking too narrowly. I had to fly through the window to get the plant. I had to potentialize.

So now I had this plant but had no business to fill it. Then I had a brainstorm: I thought, Who needs capacity more than Coca-Cola? So I set up a meeting with Neville Kirchmann, the president of Coca-Cola's Canadian operation. I explained my situation. I said, "You don't have the capacity to make enough Coke, so give me a contract for five years to make Coke, and I'll give you a good deal and that will help you to get the capacity that you need. And I'll make sure you get the kind of product that you want and you can avoid spending your capital on another plant." He agreed to a six-million-cases-a-year contract.

They gave us the product, the syrup, and the cans and everything else to complete the job. But the best part of this was that I was able to go to my other customers and tell them to drop by my plant at three o'clock. And they'd come at three o'clock to see all these red Coke cans rolling down the line. Their expressions were hilarious. So we had a good plant and around nine million cases a year of volume. We closed the other two plants in Concord and on Lakeshore Boulevard.

I sensed that Royal Crown Cola could play a role in all this. Sam had been called out of the blue in 1989 by a Royal Crown executive in Columbus, Georgia. Canada Dry had been the bottler for Royal Crown in Canada, but they had been bought by Cadbury Schweppes, which had a deal with Coke. That created a conflict, so they needed a bottler in Canada. We took over the RC franchise for Quebec in 1989 and picked up the Ontario franchise the next year.

I began to wonder if we could use the syrup to improve our flavour profile for our private-label customers. I'm the first one to admit that the old Cott cola was awful. When I was a kid, my dad used to take Cott cola and Coke and switch them in a glass. It was hilarious. As if we couldn't tell the difference. Royal Crown is the only other major producer of cola syrup besides Coke and Pepsi. It tastes sweeter than Coke but has more cola flavour than Pepsi. When you put the three of them in a taste test, Royal Crown comes out the winner most times. But Royal Crown was seen to be the poor cousin in cola because it didn't have a clue how to market itself. Cola is a business built on marketing. The product all tastes pretty much the same, so that's the only way you can distinguish yourself. Coke became the giant by controlling distribution channels. Pepsi was an also-ran until the 1940s, while RC just lagged.

In November 1990 we went off to Intra-Bev, the big annual beverage convention in Las Vegas. I glad-handed anyone I could, making connections, trying to learn. I set up a meeting with the president of Royal Crown, who was staying at the Hilton. Russ, Sam, and I went over there. And all the Royal Crown big guys were there. I went in and impressed them with our capacity and distribution. It wasn't exactly the distribution and capacity we had then. I was potentializing. They were mesmerized. If they had called us on any of it, we would have been deep in you-know-what.

I wanted to know if we could sell RC through direct store delivery if we improved the quality and the perception of private-label soft drinks. At the same time I was talking to people in the industry about the potential of using the Royal Crown concentrate in private label and whether it would help us. They said we'd never get it. Meanwhile, things were beginning to cook. I would have two hundred ideas a day. Sam went out on sales calls. Mark started making cold calls and developing the Cott-RC franchise. I worked on our operations in Montreal and Atlantic Canada, solidifying the base business. Steve Stavro of Knob Hill Farms, a big Toronto supermarket, gave us our first big break. He listed both Cott and RC Cola. Steve is one of the fine gentlemen. He liked me and wanted me to succeed. That got us going in Ontario.

Then came the breakthrough. I saw a chance to leverage it all up a level with Dave Nichol of Loblaw, which was owned by George Weston, the huge food conglomerate, run by his son, Galen. Loblaw Companies ran the biggest chain of supermarkets in the country. Nichol was a household name because he had masterminded an upscale in-store brand called President's Choice. Before President's Choice, private-label goods were considered inferior to national brands. But Nichol was a gourmand and a stickler for quality. He introduced more than twenty-five hundred private-label products for Loblaw. His first innovation was a line called No Name, products equivalent to national brands, but cheaper. Then he came up with President's Choice, which took everything up a notch in terms of quality. He introduced things to supermarket shoppers like extra-virgin olive oil, balsamic vinegar, gourmet dog food, and great cookies. He was a true showman, but he also understood the economics of the business. That's really why President's Choice was so brilliant. By controlling the manufacturing, they could make higher profit. Supermarket margins are ridiculously low—something like 0.5 to 2 per cent on sales. About the time I met him the Loblaw private-label products had sales of about $1 billion a year.

Cola was the one category Dave had never cracked, and it really drove him nuts. Cola had always been a sore spot for retailers generally. That's because of the lock Coke and Pepsi have on the world's soft-drink market. Soft drinks are about 3 to 4 per cent of supermarket sales, on average, which makes it the largest single category in the supermarket business. As a result both Coke and Pepsi had become very arrogant toward the retailer, thinking that stores needed them more than they needed stores. The joke was that retailers never made money on the category. But they needed it to bring people to the store. The whole dynamic of it made for a confrontational relationship between the retailer and the supplier.

Sam had met with Nichol in 1987. Dave was famous in the industry for his bully tactics with suppliers. That's how he kept prices down and Loblaw margins high. He gave Sam an order for about $300,000. Not long after that, Sam was at a Drexel Burnham golf tournament in Pebble Beach when he got a call from one of our people telling him that Loblaw had pulled the order. Sam hightailed it back to Toronto and tried to get in contact with Nichol. But Nichol wouldn't take his calls. Finally he called Doug Lunau, who headed up purchasing for Loblaw. Doug told him that Coca-Cola had come in with a better offer to produce their private-label cola and had put money down on the table.

I had to give Coca-Cola credit for having the brains to see the potential threat of a third manufacturer. Lunau tried to give Sam hope. "Look, Sam," he said, "hang in there. It's just a matter of time before the relationship with Coke breaks down. Their priority is going to be filling their own orders." And, sure enough, he was right. It was a hot summer, which meant that soft-drink consumption went up, which meant that Coke was running at full capacity. So Sam and Lunau did a deal with Nichol. They came up with a product they called "Cola for the Connoisseur."

But Dave was never happy with the formulation. Not long

after I started at Cott, Sam and I went to meet with him in his office on the ninth floor of the Weston Tower at Yonge and St. Clair in Toronto. He was about a half-hour late. I didn't know then that he made a point of keeping suppliers waiting. He needs to make a grand entrance. There was a cast of thousands present. On our side, Russ Plawiuk and my brother Sam. On Nichol's team was Don Watt, who masterminded Loblaw packaging. Don sat through the meeting, sketching. Jean Palmier, who handled the cola category for President's Choice, was there too.

Nichol was reasonably nice to me, in fact, probably because I wasn't like his average vendor who sat there and took a lot of crap from him. We started off by talking about doing a product like Koala Springs. But the real reason he wanted to talk to us was the cola. He told me he was fed up with this category that couldn't make any money. So I asked him what he wanted. He was pretty explicit. "You need to do three things," he said. "Number one, the product tastes like hell; two, the packaging looks like hell; and, last but not least, I want it priced 30 per cent below the national brands. Can you put all that together?" He probably expected me to cower. But I told him I could and left.

I came back to him with samples of the Royal Crown cola. I had a concept I had picked up from my experience on the Onex board. For a while Onex owned Beatrice Canada, which owned Colonial Cookies, in Kitchener, Ontario. Colonial produced cookies for the President's Choice program, including the Decadent Chocolate-Chip Cookie, which was a huge success. It outsold Chips Ahoy at Loblaw stores.

I suggested to Nichol that he could do the same thing with soft drinks. Cola offered even more potential. Then I told the RC story. I talked about it beating Coke and Pepsi in blind taste tests. Nichol loved that. I impressed on him that I could get the same syrup. More likely it would be the concentrate provided by bottlers for the private label. But it was a great story, and Dave loves a great story. He liked the RC Cola sample but made more demands about the taste. He wanted more acidity, carbonation, citrus tone, more body in the syrup. So we amended the formulation. Then I called Al Burke at RC. I told Burke I could add another 50 million cases of volume to his business. They were only selling about 150 million at the time so another 50 was pretty serious.

The only problem was that I wasn't any closer to getting the rights to the RC formula. So I made an appointment to see him, and Victor Posner, who owned Royal Crown in those days. Posner was a famous character. He was brutal, one of the most feared corporate predators on Wall Street. In the mid-1980s, he was worth about $4 billion. Half of his financing came from Drexel. And when Mike and Lowell went down, Posner was named as a co-conspirator. At this time he ran a company called DWG Corporation, which owned Arby's, Royal Crown Cola, and National Propane.

In January I got an appointment with Posner in Miami. My brother Sam and Mark Benadiba came along. Posner's offices were in a fleabag hotel on Collins Avenue that hadn't been used as a hotel for twenty years. His company had two or three floors of offices, and the rest of it was torn out. It was like being in a war zone. Overhead wires were dangling from the ceiling. Asbestos ceiling tiles were falling off.

I arrived on time for my three o'clock meeting. His people told me that I had to wait, and they put me in a little apartment within that sea of a mess. I didn't know what to expect. I had heard a bit about him but I waited for two hours, then three hours. Finally I got a message that Mr. Posner couldn't meet with me then, but if I waited until eight o'clock, he would have dinner with me and Al Burke, Royal Crown's president. Around seven-thirty, Burke came to see me in this little suite. He told me we had to wait to be notified where we're going to meet because Mr. Posner had to go to a different place every day for security reasons because he was afraid of being assassinated.

Finally we got the call. We met at Christine Lee's, a very nice Chinese restaurant. I arrive and there's this round table that seats twelve people. They never knew exactly how many would show up. The table was surrounded by no fewer than twelve security guards, with guns, real machine guns. And in the middle of it was the great Mr. Victor with his back to the wall because he was totally paranoid he was going to be shot in the back. He figured that if he sat that way he could only get shot from the front, which isn't any more reassuring, if you ask me.

Posner was this small, shrivelled little man with grey hair and a craggy face. Maybe five-foot-eight, no more than 130 pounds. He was wearing an old rumpled cashmere sweater that he bought about thirty years ago. He had two women on either side of him, like these trophy *Playboy* women, who weren't more than twenty years old. They both had outfits cut down to there and up to there. One breast flowing this way, one breast flowing that way. There was also another woman who'd been his manager for many years. Then there was a meek little accountant who was sitting across from him, telling him what happened with his stock trades for the day—how much he made and how much he lost. There was also a lawyer, who was just along for the ride. And then Mr. Posner's granddaughter from the first wife was visiting. She was going to Brown University at that time. And finally me and Sam.

Posner was drinking a bottle of Crown Royal and was really

in the pail. Every tenth word he'd nod off. Of course the guy was something like seventy-five years old, so he's entitled to doze off. But never did he not hear a word that you said. So I'm telling him about this private-label thing in Canada and the potential of the deal with Loblaw. To him Canada was some place on Pluto. But I wanted the rights to the concentrate. I had to find a connection. Obviously Milken was a sore point, so I stayed away from that. I even tried to talk to him a bit about our working on a deal with the Wegmans supermarket chain, which is based in Rochester, New York.

I hung around Miami for more than a week. We did about three of these dinners. And we negotiated the deal. Then he signed it. At that time it was for five years renewable, which gave Cott the exclusive private-label rights to his products for North America for twenty-five years. We had the right to use the RC concentrate in private-label manufacturing throughout the world.

Over the next three weeks I put together the supply agreement for the technology with RC. The next task was to improve the packaging of the Loblaw cola. This is when Don Watt entered my life. Nichol sent me to meet him at his office, the Watt Group. We clicked right away. I know how important packaging was. That's what differentiated cola. Watt is a legend in consumer packaging. He designed products for Nestlé like Nescafé coffee, Kraft, Salada. He had also designed stores. He worked for Filene's Basement in Boston, D'Agostino's in New York, Home Depot. In the early 1970s, when Galen Weston took over running Loblaw supermarkets, Watt redesigned the stores for him. He also did the packaging for the No Name and President's Choice products. The amazing thing about Don is that he is colour-blind. He wanted to be a pilot in the air force, but they wouldn't let him because of it. Don is a great salesman.

One of his favourite sayings is "Perception is reality." Don is one of the most ethical people I've worked with. He's quality all the way. World class.

We rejigged the packaging with Don's wife, Patty, a talented graphic artist. She died a couple of years ago of cancer. That was a huge loss. She was a great talent. Everyone called Patty Don's "secret weapon." Don has a lot of good ideas, but she knew how to execute them. She was a brilliant draftsperson and a great photographer. They created a change of the name or a sub-branding of the name to PC for President's Choice. We used the same colour of red that Coke uses on its can.

Then I got in touch with Crown Cork and Seal in Philadelphia, a packaging company that had always believed in my dad and the company. They gave us a hell of a price on cans, which made us competitive. So I went back to Dave. We signed the contract in March 1991. It was a multi-year contract to supply Loblaw and well as companies Loblaw supplied to. That was unprecedented. They didn't like to sign contracts with suppliers. They liked to keep their options open. But I convinced Brian Davidson, who ran the procurement division at Loblaw. I really liked Brian, who died a few years ago. He was a big, burly guy who came from the meat business, so we had a lot in common right away. With our product, Loblaw had margins as high as 20 per cent. On Coke or Pepsi, their margins were 5 per cent.

Tom Stafford at National Grocers came up with the idea to put vending machines in the stores so people could sample Cott products. That was a huge success and became another thing we could offer retailers. We now have about thirty thousand of them in the United States.

Dave Nichol gave it the big sell on the front page of the June *Insider's Report*, their popular store flyer. The price was fantastic. A 750 mL bottle of PC Cola sold for 49 cents compared with 79 cents for Coke or Pepsi. A case of twenty-four cans sold for $4.99 versus $6.99 for the big brands. Nichol did everything he could to make the cola a success. He went on television. His slogan became "If you can't taste the difference, why pay the difference?" He called the cola his "crown jewels." We also began producing other flavours for them. They just flew off the shelves. The cola became the best-selling President's Choice product. Nichol loved to boast about it.

For us, it meant we could start packaging the PC success story and sell it. We were able to tell A&P their products were inferior. We did the same thing at Oshawa Group. Everyone wanted a house-brand cola. Everyone wants to copy a winner. We were building the business and grabbing as much volume as we could. I told my people that every time you see a groundhog, you shoot his head off. If we saw a competitor, we shot his head off. We bought out our competition in Ontario, then set out buying out our competition across the country. We bought Atlantic Refreshments down east and Happy Pop in Calgary.

I began to sense that God had given me another chance. And I wasn't going to ruin this. I wasn't going to have any fancy trappings like planes or lavish offices. I was going to keep focused. I would go around the office at night, and if there were messages people hadn't returned to customers, boy, I would let them have it the next day. You have to keep your foot on the accelerator because the minute you take it off, you go back to being where everyone else is.

May 1991 was a huge month for us. We got our first big break in the United States. We had been working on landing a contract with Wegman's, a regional supermarket chain, for months. Jim White, a food consultant who had worked for

Nichol in the early 1980s developing President's Choice products, introduced us. He had developed some private-label products for Wegman's. We went into the presentation for the contract in full court press. The Watt Group talked about the need for an upscale retailer brand. Mark Benadiba did the story about operational issues, like cost and delivery. Everything went great. They were about to sign.

Then Benadiba, who was doing the negotiating, told me there were two glitches. The first was the Wegman's logo, a stylized W, which the Watt Group had designed. At Wegman's they were afraid that it looked like the PC logo. The second thing is that they wanted a lower price. I told him if Loblaw has a problem, we won't do it. I made him get permission. Fortunately Nichol was okay with it. Then they wouldn't sign until I came to the meeting. They loved me. We got on a cell phone with Fraser and banged back and forth about the price.

Wegman's cola was a huge success. We started with 200,000 cases a year and before long were producing two million. After Wegman's, we became a news story in America. Wegman's became our model. We told other retailers that if a small chain like Wegman's with fifty-five stores could sell two million cases, just think of all of the pop you can sell. In May we also opened our U.S. headquarters in Columbus, Georgia, to develop accounts. It was only a hundred miles from Coca-Cola headquarters in Atlanta. We still didn't have production in the U.S. We were supplying to Wegman's and First National from our plants in Toronto. We set up a lab in Columbus, Georgia, and hired Prem Vermani, who was the head of technical services at RC, to handle flavour technology. He had also worked for Coca-Cola for many years.

W. J. Barrs was running our fledgling program in the United

States. He was our first U.S. employee. His real name was Wilson but everybody called him W.J. He was a Southern-gentleman type. Without him our explosion into U.S. wouldn't have happened. He knew RC from the inside, having put together their bottling network.

The RC deal gave us access to forty or so independent bottlers in the U.S. My idea was that we could build a virtual company, exploiting unused capacity in other people's factories. We secured low-cost production deals by paying favourable rates to use up bottlers' excess capacity. There would be no bricks or mortar.

The early days were tough. We lost the business at Steinbergs when the company went bust. We were hustling every day. It could be a tough business. I walked in on Benadiba one day to find him on the phone with an executive from Loblaw who was chewing him out for getting an order wrong or something. I had to get in the middle of it. This was our largest customer abusing the hell out of my people. Mark told me there might have been some truth in what the guy was saying. Even so, I didn't like it. I said to the guy from Loblaw, "You know, if you don't believe we're the right kind of supplier, you have the right to pull your business, but you don't have the right to abuse my people." And he cooled down. And we worked it out.

In June I brought Fraser Latta in full-time as chief operating officer. Fraser kept us focused on a strong balance sheet. And while we disagreed at times, there are very few things I can think of that we haven't had consensus on.

Then came our next break, big time. We got a call from Steve Bailey at Wal-Mart. He asked us to fly down to their headquarters in Bentonville, Arkansas, to talk about producing Wal-Mart's new house-brand cola, a line they would call Sam's American Choice.

That connection came about because of Don Watt, who had been working with Sam Walton for more than ten years. He had done packaging for them, and designed their Store of the Future in Palmdale, California. Watt had introduced the idea to Walton that Wal-Mart should consider producing a line of private-label food, using the success of President's Choice as the example. He had even brought Loblaw into the consultation process.

So I flew down to Wal-Mart with Fraser and W.J. Barrs. I was amazed at how ordinary it looked. Here was the biggest retailer in the world, and its offices looked like a converted warehouse with forty or fifty metal chairs for suppliers to sit in while they wait for their moment. We talked to a half-dozen people. Everyone seemed enthusiastic about our supplying their soft drinks. There was only one problem: we didn't have the infrastructure to deliver the product. I had to go through another window. But I've learned in life that sometimes you can promise the truth before it happens. It's like the truth is dormant until you make it, until you will it. Around Labour Day 1991 we got the order to supply eighteen hundred stores for a November launch. It was crazy. Wal-Mart had a strict Made in the U.S.A. policy and we didn't have any real production in the U.S. That might have intimidated some people. But what did we have to lose? Nothing. There's no risk if there's nothing to lose. And what did we have to win? Everything.

In the next two months, we put together a network to get us into forty-eight different states. It was a mad rush. W.J. hired people and we used unused capacity in the RC distribution system, because they were forbidden to make private label. So suddenly all these tertiary bottlers became our co-packers.

The launch generated a lot of publicity, and gave us instant credibility in the U.S. Wal-Mart was the leader. And everyone wants to follow the leader. We were named Wal-Mart's "Supplier of the Year" in 1992. That was one of the proudest accomplishments in my career. That November we also signed contracts with Topco in Chicago and A&P Canada. At A&P we worked out a calendar for special promotions. That had never been done by a private-label manufacturer. We also negotiated for a five-year contract, which had never been done either. No one had asked. But I told my people to ask. A&P agreed.

At the beginning of 1991 we were supplying four retailers. By the end of the year we had thirty-eight. Cott products were outselling Coke and Pepsi in most of the stores we were in. Investors were starting to take notice. The stock was put on the TSE 300 Composite. It split three for one in December. In January 1992 we bought Bessey Juices in Montreal and signed Jewel Food Stores of Chicago.

About that time Brian Davidson at Loblaw called me to ask whether I'd be interested in investing in Don Watt's company. Watt had been looking for a partner. He had a lot of talent, but he wasn't great at running the day-to-day business. Don had talked to Loblaw about taking a stake, but Loblaw's president, Dick Currie, wasn't interested. Not long after that, I woke up one night, realizing what a strategic resource the Watt Group could be. That could offer a point of difference. We wouldn't simply offer pop, we could offer product development, package design, marketing, even store layout. We could become a marketing company that could help retailers generate more profit. That would be our added value.

The Watt Group didn't represent a lot of profit to a company like ours. But who cared if it ever made any money? The average businessman wouldn't look at it that way, but I did. In January 1992 we acquired a 49 per cent interest in the Watt Group, and

Don Watt came on the Cott board. In 1993 we upped our stake to 72 per cent and subsequently acquired the minority interest. I gave Watt a little bit of stock in our company, which was worth a couple of million at that time. I figured that Watt's business would improve because of the business Cott would give it. "Watty," which is what his friends called him, was happy because he didn't have to worry about money. He could continue to do his job. Brian Davidson was happy to see us buy it.

I knew that if Cott was going to succeed in a major way, we would have to change the ground rules for the way retailers viewed us. Just being a revolutionary against these two monsters, Coke and Pepsi, wouldn't be enough, because they'd bury us. The picture was coming together, in no small part because of my new friendship with Dave Nichol. After the PC Cola took off, Nancy and I began socializing with Dave and his wife, Terri, who is a very nice woman. In the beginning, Dave used to invite me for fancy dinners at the Founders Club at Toronto's SkyDome. But as soon as he'd got the last of his dessert in his mouth, he and Terri would stand up and walk out without saying a word. He'd just leave people sitting there. The second time he pulled this, I went to him and said, "You might be my biggest customer, but I don't want anything to do with you on a social basis." That was difficult for me because I hate confrontation. I don't think anyone talked to him that way before. He was speechless, but he wouldn't apologize. So then he called me again. And he kept calling me. I said no for a while. Then I agreed, and he was very polite. And we ended up becoming great friends.

On the surface, you probably couldn't find two different guys. He was a WASP from small-town Ontario, and I was a Jewish street kid from Montreal. I come across soft. He can be abrasive. But we both love to eat and laugh. And we both hate ordinary minds. He became like a brother to me. I couldn't find enough people I could talk to who would stimulate me the way he could. Dave is interested in innovation. A lot of people say that we both think outside the box. But that's not accurate. For us, there was no box to think outside. We didn't think in terms of limitations. He suggested we get into alternative beverages and iced teas. In 1992 we introduced a clear fruit drink for Loblaw called Free and Clear, which was a huge success.

I like way-out people. That's a disease I have. I like people who think they're the Messiah. That was Dave. He was messianic in fighting the supremacy of the big brands. He liked to talk about the "brand tax," which is the premium brands charged consumers just to buy their brand name. But I guess what I liked about him the most is how fragile he is. He was like this baby adult. He appealed to the father in me. He needed someone who would look after him.

The whole concept for Retailer Brands sort of evolved as the result of what Nichol and Watt were saying. We adopted the term *Retailer Brands* to distinguish ourselves from the mediocrity and lousy quality everyone associated with private-label goods. The problem with private-label products in the past was that they usually didn't have retailer commitment. National brands would come into the stores to stock merchandise and promote for the retailer. My thinking was that if we could create profitable programs for in-store retailer brands, we would create a strategic relationship with retailers. We could offer retailers advice and help in areas where they had not had a lot of success in the past. We set about trying to create customer loyalty to the store in ways that were quantifiable. By developing their own retailer brands, we told store owners, you increase the dollar value per checkout. A hidden but very real benefit of carrying our products was that they provided leverage for retailers to negotiate lower prices with Coke and Pepsi.

We had Patti and Don on the packaging work. We hired Ray Goodman, this computer wizard, to put in systems. We hired Jim White to look after food product development. We could take him into places and say this is the guy who helped to create thousands of President's Choice products. He can help you with your own house line. Retail Brands gave our preferred customers the best and brightest in packaging and retail support, as long as they kept upping their soft drink orders. Costs were basically included in the price of our soft drinks. Retailers didn't pay for it; we took it out of our margins. It probably cost us $10 million a year, which wasn't much relative to the size of the business.

I brought Heather Reisman into the company as president in July 1992. Heather had been consulting to us for a while through her company, Paradigm, and had come up with some good ideas. When she was consulting, Heather made some recommendations I acted on. One was that we take a stake in Murphy's Potato Chips, a tiny company that produced President's Choice chips. We took 60 per cent in 1992. It was also a bit of a favour to Galen Weston. Joseph Murphy, who owned the company, was his brother-in-law; he was married to Hilary Weston's sister Josephine. Joe is really clever, but he had been on the edge of bankruptcy. I liked Joe. And it didn't hurt that snack food had some of the highest profit margins in the supermarket.

Heather also advised us to buy a 25 per cent stake in Menu Foods, a terrific company that produces private-label dog and cat food. It had almost half penetration in supermarkets in Canada, as well as a bit in the United States and overseas. Menu is run by a great guy named Robert Bras, who developed some wild products with Dave Nichol such as President's Choice Gourmet Italian Dog

Food. I tasted it once in their lab. It wasn't half bad. We also bought nearly three-quarters of Lakeport Brewing, a little brewery in Hamilton, in July 1992, Dave Nichol convinced me to buy it. In the beginning we made a nice go of it. By the summer of 1993 Lakeport was producing PC Beer for Loblaw and non-alcoholic beer.

It was clear to me Heather was getting fed up with consulting, which she had done for about fifteen years. She had a great reputation in the business community, but her company was doing very poorly, in my opinion. She'd lost a few of her people. She was going nowhere. She was happy to take the job at Cott and I was glad to have her. She also opened up all sorts of new horizons like behavioural development and information technology and making Cott a learning institution. She also hooked us up with Harvard Business School to develop new operating models. Heather is very different from me in her approach. She's systematic; I'm instinctive. She likes to talk about things like "the rings," these concentric circles she had read about in a book by a Harvard professor. The inner circle was the great product. The outer ones were logistics, then all the help that we'd give to the customers, then the interdependence and how we'd layer all this on top. She called it the Total Product Service Bundle—Product, Marketing, Design.

Heather also introduced me to some good people. She brought in a guy called Stan Elbaum with her to implement systems. You've got to remember that three years earlier we didn't even own a computer. All our orders, sales plans, and calculations were done on placemats or takeout menus, whatever was around the office. She also introduced me to Humberto Aquino, who worked at the brokerage Burns Fry doing mergers and acquisitions. He came in to run Cott South America. He is a very talented guy who ended up being really useful in a bunch of areas.

At Cott I always looked to hire people who could potentialize, people willing to go the extra distance, who believed. By believed, I mean people who believed that the company could make a difference. Otherwise you have nothing. Sometimes I got criticism for hiring so many smart young kids and paying them a lot. My thinking is that tomorrow they'll come up with a great new idea.

We started talking about becoming the General Foods of retail brands. The thinking was that we would look for high-profile categories that would add to the quality perception of the store. Retailers would be able to increase their margins while decreasing prices. We offered them a unique strategic relationship. It was an unbeatable combination. I developed that notion, and then I used Heather to execute it. And she did a great job. Inside Cott we called the approach "The Look, The Taste, The Plan!" Heather liked to call us a New Age company and Cott's New House. When we took over a category it was to Cott-icize it. The company felt like a family. We knew that we were breaking ground. We were change makers. We weren't merely a factory. Our job was to help our customers redefine their businesses and gain competitive edge. That became a big part of the company's value.

The big breakthrough in our public image came in September 1991 in an article in *Forbes* titled, "Hell no, we won't pay! Why consumers are no longer faithful to their favorite brands." It gave Cott big play: "To beat pros like Coke or Pepsi at its own game is an amazing feat for Cott and an object lesson for those who believe that brand loyalty is guaranteed." The article reflected the prevailing thinking. National brands had come under the microscope. They had seen explosive growth in profits in the 1980s, but in the 1990s they didn't seem to represent the same value. Prices had risen while the product quality had declined. But with the advent of retailer brands, they were seeing market share and margins shrink. Some of them came back with price reductions and promotions. In some cases, they came out with their own private label.

We benefited hugely from the surrounding hype. We were signing one or two new accounts every month or two. And to be honest there wasn't much else happening in the market at that time, so you get a good writer and top-notch readership looking at the potential demise of brands, and it was dynamite for us.

Before long investment analysts were taking notice. Some of the big national brands' stock prices were slumping. And they started predicting the increase of private-label market share. The increase in our stock price didn't have a lot to do with our success in Canada, other than with some of the hype associated with President's Choice. It really exploded when we started to serve customers in the U.S. and when the Wal-Mart news got out. Then it became a real North American story and had a lot more interest from American investors than the Toronto Stock Exchange investors. We were listed on NASDAQ in June 1992. That's where 90 per cent of the activity in our stock over the past few years has been.

Cott was a growth story and Americans are more responsive to that than Canadians. In Canada they said, "Here's another real fast-track story, another Pencer story." It was diluted by the Financial Trustco experience. Institutional investors in Canada weren't interested in the stock. Royal Trust bought stock off and on, and they've made money with it. But there's a real wait-and-see attitude about things in Canada. Now we're getting more play in Canada because there's more Canadian investors interested in buying our stock.

Lessons from the Master Salesman

The first thing you have to be able to do is to be comfortable with whoever you have to deal with, no matter what their position is. I can go and deal with the biggest account and deal one day with Galen Weston, the billionaire chairman of George Weston, which owns Loblaw. The next day with Brian Davidson, the next day with Dave Nichol, then the buyers, then the store managers, and then the guy who wraps up the parcels. I'm not happy if I can't get into your head. Maybe it's just that I'm a busybody. I want to know everything and I enjoy being part of someone else's life.

A big mistake people make is trying to appeal to people at their levels or higher, thinking that's the way up the ladder. They call it "managing up." But I always felt that the people at the lowest end of the ladder have the most ability to help you because that's where things are done. That's how products are sold. They're not sold by Galen Weston. They're sold by the guy who fills the shelves. The whole system fails if you don't have the support of all the players. And I was good at making sure that nobody destroyed this thing. I was good at co-opting everybody to be behind it.

You have to create a relationship with the customer that's unique, a relationship that your competitor is unwilling or unable to do. That's our definition of marketing—creating a strategy that your competitor is unwilling or unable to follow. But how do you do that? We work very hard with our customer to not just look at what they sell in soft drinks but to help them to improve the overall profitability of the store, by having people who understand how we can bring value in many more areas, whether it's developing packaging, or figuring out how to make more money for them. Some people just say, "Well, you gave it away." Other people would say, "You've built your business on that." There are two ways of looking at it. You wouldn't have a business without doing that because that was the business, that was the idea. And that's the crucial point in our success in keeping our customers: having all the best services or having the best logistics, or having a lot of these things that we bring that nobody brings in any business that I know of.

Sure, all these services reduce our potential profit, but there's a more important benefit, creating interdependence. That's when the customer understands that you bring a lot more than 10 cents a case at a lower price. And that creates a longer-term relationship. But you have to keep it up. This is a business based on "what did you do for me yesterday?" It's not easy.

What I brought to Cott is the vision that we really want to share with the customer. The brands' big mistake was that they were selfish. They were unwilling to invest money with the customer they might not have a direct return on. It's hard even to convince my own people. Since I've been running Cott, we must have given away $50 million in packaging and advice.

This is a business where the retailers, not the manufacturers, own the shelves. What we need to own, or what we need to own half of, is this interdependence. If there's no interdependence, we're just a manufacturer. I would go to a customer and say, "Look, I have an idea for you that will let you double your drink sales. You're going to make more money, but you've got to do things in a different way, and we're going to help you to do that." And they'd say, "Well, it sounds good, but we don't want to take the risk." And we'd say we'd also provide them with $1 million or something to promote their product. No private-label company ever helped the customer to promote a private-label product and defer it and let it be paid out over the life of the contract.

126

Take vending machines. Cott is probably the third-biggest vending-machine company in the world. We have thirty thousand vending machines in the United States. We invested $30 million in vending machines. Until this year I don't think we've made any money. Only this year we're finally turning a profit.

My big challenge is to help management be at the leading edge, far ahead of its competition. There's no science to it but a lot of art. There's a different personality for each customer, but you have to interpose a strategy partner into the relationship or one or two or three or four, depending on different abilities that the company has.

And that's where we stung Coke and Pepsi. The president of Safeway listened to us. The president of Wal-Mart listened to us. Coke and Pepsi had no time to meet with them. There was always a confrontational attitude between Coke, Pepsi, and retailers. Coke and Pepsi have been teaching them how not to make money for twenty years. We forced Coke and Pepsi to become more in tune with the customers' needs.

Gerry Pencer's Art of the Deal

A good deal maker learns to understand what the person across the table wants. That's a very big skill. It sounds simple, but it's not. You don't sell them what you want to sell. Most people, that's the way they operate. They want to sell an idea so they walk in and say, "Here's the idea." You have to be able to listen to the music. In 1996 I sent Mark Benadiba off to buy Texas Beverage Packers Inc. in San Antonio. But I couldn't stay away. I managed to be in San Antonio on the final day of the negotiations. They had hit a snag. It was an insignificant thing. The other side wanted some concessions about a long-time employee. This was a multimillion-dollar deal, but Mark wasn't prepared to give. I had a sixth sense about it. I walked in and closed the deal. I figured out what the problem was by paying attention. He was dealing with nuts and bolts. You have to be able to listen to the music.

You've got to see every person you approach as a new custom-made suit. People don't want a ready-made suit, they want a custom-made suit. That's very important. If a customer doesn't want pants, you don't phone him up and say, "Hey, I'm quoting this with pants." Better you should get the deal, then sell him the pants later. You do this by taking time with people, by being able to communicate with them, particularly through their eyes. Very few people can make eye contact. You're never going to sell the big picture unless you're able to do that.

Always give back half. Always leave something on the table. You don't need it all. You never need to strike the last bid. That way, the customer feels that whoever is dealing with him has power. Share with the customer so that he can feel good about this deal too. It's the smartest investment he can make. You don't destroy your opponent to make a new deal. "The bulls win, the bears win, the pigs they never win." That's what I tell my people. Also remember that the word *no* is not in your vocabulary. People lose so many deals because they say no. They don't realize there's always a way to get around no, a way to make the people you're negotiating with feel comfortable, to let them feel that you're really listening.

How did I get Wal-Mart? I couldn't say no. If I had been practical, I wouldn't be doing business with them, because I had no way of serving them. But you never say no. I am not a gam-

Gerry with his Mom and Dad in Montreal. (1947)

Gerry, David Boltuc and Sam Rubin at the opening of Curly Joe's
Restaurant in Montreal, 1971.

Financial Trustco Days. Bill Tanner, future Premier of Alberta Ralph
Klein (then mayor of Calgary) and Gerry. (1980)

Gerry and his father, Harry Pencer. (1982)

Great times with friends Larry Tanenbaum and Gerry Schwartz.
(1992)

Gerry and Dave Nichol in Japan with sumo wrestler Aki Bono and
his assistant-in-training. (1993)

Nancy and Gerry in Sardinia, Italy. (1992)

The family Christmas vacation: David, Gerry, Clarke, Nancy, Stacey and Holly. (1993)

Gerry with grandson, Jesse, doing their favorite thing together—look at their facial expressions. (1995)

Gerry enjoying being a "Papa" with Joshua in 1996.

Gerry with his "boys": David, Jesse and Clarke.

Gerry with his good friends, Lawrence and Fran Bloomberg, two weeks after surgery in June 1997.

Best friends: Gerry and his son-in-law David in 1994.

Gerry and Clarke having fun together on Father's Day, 1997. It was Gerry's last.

Gerry and Mark Benadiba at the 1997 Annual General Meeting.

August 1997, Gerry's audience with the Pope.

Holly speaking about her
Dad on Capitol Hill in 1997.

A group shot of the patient and family advising committee during
construction of the Pencer Brain Tumor Centre. (1998)

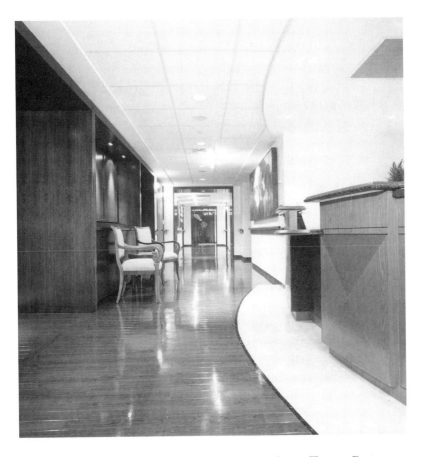

The entrance at the Gerry and Nancy Pencer Brain Tumor Centre.

The hallway at the Gerry and Nancy Pencer Brain Tumor Centre.

A juice bar at the Gerry and Nancy Pencer Brain Tumor Centre.

bler in the sense of going to Las Vegas. There's a big difference between being a gambler and walking on the ledge. A person who walks on the edge has two inches on each side of his shoe, so therefore you can't afford any mistakes or he's down. A person who walks on the ledge has maybe four or six inches on either side of him, so he needs to be deliberate but he's not quite at the same height as the person who's walking right on the ledge. In some of my antics I was on the edge when I was younger, but I wouldn't describe myself that way for the past fifteen or twenty years. I'm always imagining that I can do what I need to do, so I don't need to gamble to do that.

We had an elephant by the tail with Cott. We had everything to offer the customer. And every retailer felt it was fashionable to deal with us. I was always craving the next big ride, the next home run. After Wal-Mart our next major success was signing on Safeway in December 1992. Loblaw was the most significant deal in terms of getting credibility. Wal-Mart the most important in terms of profile. But philosophically Safeway was the closest we would get to the vision of an integrated, interdependent relationship. We developed hundreds of products for them.

We were on a comet. In 1992 we signed Zellers in Canada, and Fred Meyer, Smiths and Randall's in the U.S. The next year we signed Kmart Australia, Makro and Pick 'N Pay South Africa, Kmart, Lucky Stores, and Southland 7-Eleven in the U.S. We were supplying more than ninety retail chains, and we had a waiting list. We literally could not handle the business. We were suddenly dealing with customers on the basis that we would give them pickup within two hundred miles of any point in the

United States or we'd pay the freight. It was crazy, but it gave us a competitive advantage because none of these other folks would be able to compete on a national basis. Earnings and revenues were doubling. We moved early the next year into beautiful offices in the Queen's Quay terminal overlooking Lake Ontario.

Our annual meeting in June 1993 was like a revival meeting. I taped it so all our employees could see it. By then we had more than three hundred people working for us, including several members of my family.

I clipped a mike to my jacket and walked into the crowd. I asked them how many people thought retailer-branded drinks are better than Coke and Pepsi. The crowd went wild. I told them we'd sell 150 million cases, up from 60 million the year earlier. I then brought up a bottler from Columbus to the stage and asked him how Cott helped his business. He told everyone how wonderful it was. Then Monwabisi Fandeso, a general manager from National Sorghum Breweries Limited, handling American Choice in South Africa, told how Nelson Mandela was drinking American Choice at his birthday party, not Coke or Pepsi.

By this time, a lot of my employees were starting to doze off. I got their attention by revealing a new stock plan that allowed them to buy a certain number of shares at the price it was when they joined the company. Just after that I got a note from some-body telling me to get off the stage. The meeting ended with twenty children singing "O Canada" in Cott t-shirts. I couldn't keep tears from filling my eyes. I had been there not even five years and we had created this. I had conceptualized this and made it true.

❖　❖　❖

I structured Cott by not structuring it. Titles didn't mean anything. I was number-one sales guy, involved in every deal. Every day we were making a deal, pushing a deal. Don Watt and I would go off to Wal-Mart and Safeway. Heather would say, "What's your plan?" We'd say, "We don't have one. We'll just listen to what they have to say. Then we'll come up with a plan." That would drive her crazy.

It was life in the pressure cooker, but I loved it. Every day brought great highs and lows. Every day was a long day. There was never enough time. I'd be on the phone at midnight with my people. And I'm the first to say that I could be demanding with them.

We bought the Gulfstream II in 1993. Before that we shared a plane with Schwartz, but he ended up with it. When we weren't using the plane, I was leasing it out to people like Bruce Springsteen and Elton John. It may seem like a luxury, but it wasn't, considering I was spending eight hundred hours a year in the air. I would spend almost three days a week on the road, not only visiting our customer base in North America but building relationships with retailers in Europe, Australia, and South Africa. It wasn't unusual for us to travel to San Francisco, where Safeway had its headquarters, and back in the same day. I would fly at six o'clock in the evening, have a dinner meeting with the customer, then fly home all night so I could be in the office the next morning. If I had something that was pumping me, like getting a deal finished, I could go twenty-four hours or forty hours straight. I never travelled during business hours, never. If I wanted to go to Los Angeles, I'd leave at seven o'clock in the evening and get there at eight o'clock their time. I always had a business meeting awaiting me when I got there.

It was nothing for me to fly to a meeting with Kmart in Australia, about twenty-five hours each way, to get to Melbourne from Toronto, and to only stay two and a half hours for a meeting. But I always felt if there were issues, there were tensions, I had to go. No one could substitute. I always felt that it was important to let people know they're number one, that you cared, and that you were prepared to make that commitment. Without it you don't have anything.

◆ ◆ ◆

Coke and Pepsi were effectively a duopoly. But you can't blame Coke and Pepsi for that. The best thing anyone ever said to me about monopolies was Lord Kadury, one of the richest men in the world. He owned Peninsula Hotels. He came from one of the richest families in Hong Kong. I met him in 1984. I was still at Financial Trustco and then Senator Jack Austin, who was on the board of Financial Trustco, invited me and Nancy to accompany him and his wife, Natalie, when he was given an honorary degree at the University of Macau. Jack did a lot of work in the Pacific Rim, acting for the Chinese government in creating interest in Canada for industrial investment. Pierre Trudeau also received a degree on that trip, as did Henry Kissinger. I went to a little restaurant in a casino owned by Stanley Ho that served a very sweet seafood type of Chinese food. I loved it. We were watching a group of men play a game called fan tan, which is a ridiculous game designed around a cup and beans. Lord Kadury leaned over and said to me, "Gerry, the only thing wrong with a monopoly is when you're not part of it."

So here was little Gerry in his latest incarnation, pitting him-

132

self against Coke and Pepsi, the two most sophisticated and most respected marketing machines in the world. *Fortune* magazine named Coke "the world's number-one brand" in 1993. We became the little tail wagging the dog. The first sign we were having an influence occurred in 1992. Coca-Cola Canada reported its first ever loss. It replaced Neville Kirschmann as head of the company with William Casey from its American bottling system to make the company profitable again.

We were a big problem for these guys. A really big problem. They put teams together to figure out how to handle us. Coke put one of its senior executives full-time on a task force dealing with Cott. It was all over the industry. It was called Operation Parasite. In October 1994, at an industry trade show, Douglas Ivester, the president of Coca-Cola, blasted us in his keynote address. He called companies like Cott parasites for bringing cheaper products to market without making investments in new products and marketing. His line was that the industry has to do something about these parasites called Cott who aren't putting any money into innovation, packaging, all the things that the national brands were doing. What he was really saying is that there's no equity in any one of the customers for any one of his brands. It gave away the fact they were really hurting. They were running scared.

They went out trying to jab away at us, saying that retailer brands weren't making a high-enough margin for the retailer because there were supposedly hidden costs, like freight and warehousing costs. This was predictable, in that our presence meant that all of a sudden they had to give a lot more services to the retailers than they had in the past. Coke and Pepsi re-engineered their businesses. Their mistake was to turn their products into commodities by getting consumers to be willing to switch for just money. They set themselves up. And then when we came out with a product that was totally indiscernible from theirs, why would anyone pay 35 per cent more for it?

They started to give the retailers more of their profit. They stopped ignoring the retailers. And last but not least, they started giving consumers a better price. Diehard Coke and Pepsi drinkers have Cott to thank for that. This is the big story here. Nobody knew how really frightened they were at that time, that billions of dollars of their market capitalization was being eroded. They were wasting all their time with this small-time espionage, setting up these committees. And finally realizing that they had to be nice to retailers who they'd been not nice to for twenty-five years.

On June 9, 1993, Pepsi shares fell 9 per cent on Wall Street, down by 3.25 to 31.50 amid panic selling, after a company statement that second-quarter earnings would be flat. In advance of the 1993 Christmas season, Pepsi dropped the price on a twenty-four-can case from $6.99 to $5.49. In November, Coca-Cola Canada announced it was laying off 560 employees, more than 10 per cent of its workforce, and closing half of its sixteen plants. Then Pepsi launched what it called an "all-out" assault with a bunch of new products, packaging, and lower prices. Like Coke, they were cutting their workforce and restructuring operations. By the end of 1993 it was clear Coke and Pepsi were running scared. Private label had grown 50 per cent to a 28 per cent share of a $1.6 billion business. Pepsi was the first to panic. They dropped prices across the U.S., which is what I think really did them in against Coke. They were so worried about Cott that they forgot what they were really competing with. We were nothing, next to their clout. But even when we went into South Africa and other places, they reacted the same way.

Maybe this is paranoia on my part, but I began to feel that somebody was following me. So I went to Kroll and Associates, which is the best-known investigation service in the world. I approached them through my attorneys in New York. What was interesting was that they sent my engagement cheque back. They said they weren't willing to take on the case because of a conflicting assignment. I feel they had been retained by somebody who had a big interest in bringing me down.

I got a bit nervous about it all so I hired a guy to drive me and act as my majordomo. He told me he'd murdered his wife's dog because he was having a spat with her. When I heard that, I made sure I never got him angry. He was once with Scotland Yard, but he was more like Inspector Clouseau. He looked like him too. In that first movie, *The Pink Panther*, Clouseau goes in to check into a hotel and he says, "Do you have a rrrroom?" The hotel owner says no. Sitting beside the owner is a dog. And Clouseau says, "Does your dog bite?" And the man says no. And then Clouseau goes to play with the dog. And the dog just about takes his arm off. So Clouseau he looks at this guy and says, "I thought your dog does not bite." And the guy replies, "That is not my dog."

When I started at Cott the stock was trading for less than a quarter. By 1993 it was on its way to $50 and a market capitalization of almost $3 billion. The stock split twelve times since July 1990. Analysts were saying they'd never seen a stock appreciate as quickly. That's when the shorts came on the scene.

For those of you lucky enough never to have heard about

short sellers, they're vultures who bet on a company failing, which means that its stock price will decline. They sell shares they don't own. They hope the stock price falls so they can buy them at a lower price to fill their "short position." As long as they buy the stock back at a lower price, they're making money. It's hugely risky but it also can be hugely profitable. But what these guys do is bet on failure, and do everything they can to spread negative news. That kind of thinking is alien to me.

In the beginning, as the stock was rising, the "shorts," as they're known, lost a hell of a lot of money on Cott. The ringleaders were a couple of Canadian investors, and they sent out information to American short sellers as well. It started in December 1992, when Michael Palmer of Equity Research Associates put a sell recommendation on the stock. This is a guy whose nickname is "Mad Dog." He published a research report that suggested Cott wasn't paying its bills or suppliers. That was totally untrue. We were paying them within two weeks, when the normal terms are sixty days. And he made some other statements that were also untrue. None of the shorts' rumours amounted to anything. One of them said we were going to lose our major accounts with Wal-Mart and Loblaws. To this day, that never happened.

What I can't believe is that one of the shorts, an accounting professor at York University in Toronto, was actually teaching these things to students while he was an acknowledged seller of the stock.

There's no question Cott presented the shorts with opportunity to make a lot of money. The stock was trading at a very high multiple, especially for a Canadian stock. It was also a story stock. All private-label companies were trading at enormous multiples, whether it was us or Parigo, the private-label drug manufacturer. The hype was out there that private labels could then do no wrong.

The shorts guys are incredibly well organized. They even went out and created this fancy name—the Canadian Institute for Retired Chartered Accountants—and printed up beautiful stationery that they sent to major investors and customers of ours in the United States. It made them look like a prestigious, credible institution while they were brutally dirty and dangerous. They were sending critical reports of us to Wal-Mart every two weeks. The guys we dealt with at Wal-Mart would be calling me, asking, "What's going on here? Who are these people?" It was a total waste of everyone's time.

The shorts also attacked our accounting practices. I'm very good at the rules of general accounting. We were always very careful to comply with these rules, but if we saw an opportunity to present our financial picture in a way that more appropriately reflected reality, we'd do it. The people who read our statements knew what we were doing. There was always full disclosure. It was always perfectly kosher accounting. If you look at our balance sheet now, I say we did it exactly right. We've proven them wrong. That doesn't mean I didn't begin in an aggressive way to get there in the first place. I'm good at putting the car on the fast track. Coopers and Lybrand audited and signed my financial statements for twenty-five years, and they had a hell of a lot to lose.

It amazed me how much the shorts were able to manipulate the press. Here are five or six people who reflect the thoughts of a very tiny part of the people who follow our company. Eighty per cent of our public stock is owned by Americans, not Canadians. And everybody keeps asking the same questions. And a lot of them are unimportant to the scheme of things and to what the real investor or interested party wants to know. And for reporters to think I could have finessed this major fraud. They're unbelievable imbeciles. So much of the fuss about Cott was amateur scandal.

They also made a stink about my family selling stock. But what family business doesn't cash out from time to time? Insiders are entitled like outsiders to make a return, and I never sold any stock at more than 40 per cent of what it was at the height, never. I made money on stock options, that's true. But I haven't received a bonus in four years because results in the past few years didn't warrant it. You've got to be fair to your shareholders. Maybe because of my past, because of the shorts, because of the newspapers, all those things stuck in my mind so much that I would go overboard to go to the other extreme.

By May of 1994 I had had enough of it. I decided it was time to fight back. I launched a $14 million lawsuit against Palmer. So all of a sudden he dropped off the face of the earth as far as being a public short of Cott. By July the price had dropped from $50 to $18, thanks in large part to sustained attacks by short sellers. We also hired a professor at the University of Chicago and an extremely well-known and highly respected accounting authority to look at our books and make a report. That's what you have to do when you have all those people making unfounded allegations. He said great things about us and agreed with our accounting practices.

The thing that bothered me most was not the price of our stock. What people never focused on was that even from the lowest point our stock was eighty times what it was when I started. I felt sorry for people who had invested in this stock to have it obliterated by these shorts. What nobody talks about is how the shorts rob innocent people of the money that they should have earned with their stock by phoning the reporters and trying to get them to print lies, which they've successfully done in many cases. That's more relevant.

Publications in the U.S. like *Fortune* and *Forbes* and *USA Today* had such major pieces on Cott's success. In Canada, though, the focus was mostly on the negative—the shorts, the background of that, the fluctuation up and down of the stock. It's discouraging, but that's the way it was. A lot of people who didn't believe missed out on the big ride. At one time we had a bigger market cap than Power Corporation of Canada, the big conglomerate.

And then one day out of the blue I got a telephone call from Garrett Herman, the chief executive of the brokerage firm Loewen Ondaatje McCutcheon. He wanted to come and see me. So he showed up at my office and told me that he wanted to hire Mad Dog Palmer as his head of research, but as long as this lawsuit was hanging over him, he didn't feel he could. We wanted to make peace and asked if I was prepared to see Palmer. The average guy maybe would have just said, No, I'm not interested. But I agreed to see Palmer and Herman with Fraser. When he showed up, I called him every profanity I knew. And he just had to sit there and take it. The reality is that money, greed, motivates people to do things that they shouldn't do. He had no interest in telling investors what was really going on at Cott. He was there to make money at the expense of other shareholders. The bottom line is that he was willing to trade. I give him a release and he agrees to do his best to get these other guys off my back.

The question the press missed was: Was the company hyped too much? Did the financial press in the United States push this whole category too far? Did they create the situation for this to

139

happen, much as it did in the biotech industry? What happens is this: Analysts start pushing the stock and raising the estimate. And once a stock runs to where they've recommended it, they have two choices: they can take off the recommendation or raise it. They created expectations that we couldn't meet for their own selfish interests. And maybe we didn't give them good enough guidance, but how could you? It was very hard for us even from a month-to-month base with a company growing that fast to ever figure out where we were. We weren't General Motors. I wasn't worried about fulfilling stock-market expectations. Our job was to keep finding new customers, signing on new customers, delivering the product to the customers. Sure, if I had been more focused on that, I would have paid more attention to it. But it wasn't what was interesting to me at the time. New customers, new countries, getting my product out, selling it, delivering it. That's what turned me on.

There's no question that hype was a big part of the Cott story. Hype isn't necessarily the press. It comes from a whole bunch of different avenues. If your customers start talking about you, that's hype. If your suppliers start talking about you, if your competitors start talking about you, and the press being a very important part of that, both the business press, meaning the trade press, and the general press, that's all hype. I love hype. I'm even willing to give my publisher a few hundred thousand dollars to create a lot of noise about this book. Hype is important.

I've been told that selling twenty thousand copies of a business book in this country is considered to be a great accomplishment. So I figure I'll buy fifty thousand copies to kick it off. I'll donate it to every library in the world. But the biggest part of our hype came from all the antics of Coke and Pepsi defending themselves in the newspapers and television. That's been the biggest part of the hype that Cott could have achieved over the last six or seven years.

A high point for us was Marlboro Friday, April 2, 1993. That's when Philip Morris reduced the price of a pack of cigarettes by 40 cents in response to all the hype at the time about the high cost of brand-name products. Its stock lost about $13 billion of market value in one day. Shares of other national brands like Coca-Cola, Heinz, and Colgate-Palmolive also took a nosedive.

But the pinnacle for us was a *Fortune* story that ran in August 1993, called "Brands—It's Thrive or Die." It was a great piece for Cott. There was a big picture of me and Don Watt. We had retailers talking to us and investment dealers wanting to know more about the company. The stock was on its way to its peak. We didn't know that then, though. No one could ever afford to buy the kind of publicity, good and bad, that Cott was able to get over those years. It created excitement and a lot of momentum. I guess in hindsight I've benefited from both sides of the sword. But we've had a lot more positive stuff than negative stuff. The only place I ever got any negative stuff to any degree is in Toronto. I think there was one American magazine that used the Toronto shorts as its source for a story, but generally things in the U.S. have been more than fair. It's not just the issue of negativity in the Canadian business scene, there's also a degree of envy. Wouldn't every one of these little guys love to have my job? Wouldn't they love to change their $30,000-a-year job for mine? I think there's a big degree of that. The problem is that people feel entitled in Canada. Everybody here is entitled—entitled to free medical care, entitled to child care, to lifetime union job security. People want to level the playing field, so why not cut their legs off? The press is more than happy to provide these people with an opportunity to do that, so that's what they go out to do. In America the sense of entitlement is nowhere as high as it is here.

But power is changing. I think that the Canadian establishment as we know it is dying. They're caretaker businesses. I think there's a lot of this with the gentile establishment in Toronto, but I don't deal with them. Let them go to their little golf clubs and yacht clubs that don't include Jews. Who cares? I wouldn't go anyway. The establishment here is made up of people who can't make it on their own. They make it because they're connected to a group who tries to help each other from becoming extinct. Even Galen Weston has done more for his business than these other guys have. He at least works or tries to. He was smart at the beginning because he went out and made those decisions to hire Nichol and Currie, and he saved the company. And structuring it the way he did was brilliant, putting them on the same level, almost like two brothers and him being the father. It was an ideal, given those two guys' personalities. It was brilliant.

But I believe these things are changing, and for the better. Just look at who's running the banks—those guys are not in the establishment either. Take a guy like Peter Godsoe, the chairman of Scotiabank. I mean, this guy is a whole new type of real entrepreneur. Godsoe is one sharp guy. He's got the most profitable bank on the asset side. He's the kind of guy who had faith in me. I dealt with the Royal Bank for thirty years, but in the end they didn't understand my business. They were very nice to me, but when it came time to talk really serious money, they weren't willing to take the time to understand it. I had to switch banks and go to the Bank of Nova Scotia. And they took the time at the most senior level, not ratcheting you down forty layers to where the guy doesn't understand anything. I went to see Rick Waugh, the number-two guy at the bank. Rick gave us an $80-million line of credit. He had a lot of confidence in me.

◆ ◆ ◆

Every kid of mine has a story. Stacey is the oldest. When she was about five years old, Stacey got septic arthritis in her hip. That was very scary because they had to put her into traction and hope that the infection would go away. Even if it did, and that was a big if, the doctors were concerned that she'd be left with a limp. But she pulled through.

Stacey is like a tiger. She's a real fighter. After high school, she decided she wanted to work with children, so she enrolled in an early-childhood-education course in Calgary, which was a diploma course. She didn't have the entry marks to get into the university. Then after we moved to Toronto, she went to see the administrators of York University to try to convince them to let her into the undergraduate program to get a bachelor's degree in psychology. What chutzpah. She didn't take no for an answer. It was like something I would have done. And she convinced them. I'm sure she used all the charm she has, and all her Pencer genes. But he let her into the program and she graduated with very nice marks. I was bursting with pride at her graduation. Today her degree hangs in my office at Cott.

Stacey met David Cynamon in the summer of 1991 at a B'nai B'rith charity baseball tournament in Toronto. I didn't really start to get to know David for about six months after that. Just as I was Harry the Second, taking after my dad, David in many ways is Gerry the Second, even though he probably doesn't need the association. But it was as though another little Gerry showed up on our family's doorstep. By the time he

143

was twenty-five, David had made his first million. It's as if the clock had been turned back thirty years. Like me, he's got a big ego and he's fiercely competitive. He also likes to get involved in everybody's lives, which can be difficult. He jokes that he transformed Stacey, much like I transformed Nancy. But Stacey was always beautiful to me.

David was born in Edmonton, but moved to Toronto in 1986 when he was twenty-one, when HavInfo, the company he was running, set up business here. The way David set up HavInfo reminds me of my early days. He approached Bruce Bronfman and Steve Reichmann in Toronto to back his business. He didn't know how powerful their families were. Belzberg was the big name out west. They agreed. HavInfo began as a pretty primitive data base. It had stuff like the yellow pages on it so you could look up the nearest plumber, or movies, or stock quotes. It was ahead of its time because in those days home computers weren't as available as they are now, plus they were really expensive. He quickly realized people would buy the system for stock quotes, so they focused on that. It was listed on the Vancouver Stock Exchange and took rights to Ontario. The company was doing poorly. David took over the company, gave stock for the debt, cleaned it up, and moved it to Toronto.

David hadn't heard of Cott when he met me. It was just becoming well known in financial circles. Cott was trading at about $18, on its way up to $100. I advised him to buy some. I was positive the stock was going to $100. He thought I was some wild promoter. Actually he never bought a share until 1996, when it went down to $7 or $8.

I have to admit that I was so consumed with myself all my life that I was oblivious to everything, including him, for the first little while. But I got the message that he was a great guy with good values. Business was a big link between us. I was impressed with his moxie. I loved to pick his brain about how he set up his business, what he thought about things. I wanted David in my business. So in February 1993, I took him to visit a meat company in Calgary I was thinking of investing in. I didn't know it then, but David planned to meet with his father in Calgary to tell him he was going to ask Stacey to marry him. His dad, Henry, is very diversified in his business interests—he has hotels, restaurants, the largest vending business in Alberta, real estate, and a food-service business in a sports stadium.

On the plane on the way from Edmonton to Toronto, David lost his voice, which he does when he's nervous. He came to sit beside me and asked my permission to ask Stacey to marry him. I turned into Niagara Falls. I had to take my glasses off, they were so soaked with tears. I hugged and kissed him. And just at that moment the stewardess came out of the front cabin. David caught a glance of her out of the corner of his eye. She looked horrified. She must have thought we were lovers. It was hilarious. As soon as we landed we headed to the hospital to tell Nancy, who was recovering from back surgery. But she was so drugged that she couldn't figure out what we were saying.

Before David married Stacey, he had a gentlemen's dinner in Nassau. And we went fishing. They had baseball hats made up with "Go Big or Go Home" written on them. When he was a kid, his philosophy was do it big or don't even bother. I had never heard the expression, but it summed up my own philosophy. I don't believe in half measures. If you can't do something in a big way, don't do it at all.

Stacey and David got married in September 1993. It was a beautiful simcha. No one had a grander wedding in Toronto. Nancy did a fantastic job planning it. I brought in the Peter

Duchin Orchestra from New York. We also hired a klezmer band. There was dancing in the street. It was a wonderful night. One of my proudest as a father.

From day one, David's been sensitive to maintaining an independent identity, which I respect, though I wish he would let me help him more. When he was twenty-five and had his first taste of real success, he bought a Cartier watch. Before he married Stacey, Nancy and I wanted to buy him a gold Cartier. He didn't want it. Finally he agreed, but he wears the one he bought himself every day, and takes the present out only for special occasions. Then when I bought my Ferrari, I wanted to give my Porsche to him. He wanted it, but only if he could buy it from me.

I wanted them to live in Forest Hill near to us. So I found a house I wanted to buy as a wedding present. David wouldn't agree to that. The final deal I cut was that I paid for half and David paid for half. After they got married they decided to renovate the house, so they stayed with us. Stacey was pregnant with Jesse. Their house was ready after seven months, but they kept making one excuse or another about why they couldn't move back. They had a $1-million house across the street but they preferred to live with us. Finally they decided to wait until their baby was born. They stayed until June 5, 1994, the night Jesse was born. By coincidence it was Stacey's birthday too. David says it was the best year of his life. We had fun every minute we were together.

Stacey invited the whole family to both deliveries. That's how close we are. And it's something I'll never forget, being able to share that moment. I even cut the umbilical cord when their second son, Joshua, was born. I wasn't even in the room when my kids were born. The day Clarke was born I was opening a Curly Joe's in a mall in Montreal.

Holly is my second daughter, and a very different kind of girl. She's a real pistol. She has the most *joie de vivre* of all my kids, yet underneath she has many of the same complexities I do. She was born on my twenty-fifth birthday, so maybe it's not surprising she's the most like me. Not the least is the fact that she's a terrible driver. Once she T-boned two cars in one week, which has to be a Pencer family record. She's got a hundred things going on in her head at any time. She's the most independent and a bit of a rebel. After graduating from university, she worked for Cott for a year or two, then went to London to work for our European operation for about six months. That was a bold move for her. Then out of nowhere she decided she was going to be a chef. So she enrolled at George Brown in Toronto and she got a diploma in cooking. Why she did that, I have no idea. If you asked her, she would probably say neither does she. Then she started to work for us at Cott, and she was very good.

She set up the "Stars and Stripes" program for us in the United States. That's a brand for retailers who are too small to have their own house retailer brand. It includes juices, water products, and soft drinks, stuff like that. It's a great defence mechanism. She put together a small team and realized my vision. And from nothing it's now contributing a lot of profit. She started that in January 1997. This year it's already selling about five million cases a year.

Clarke is my hero. He's stood up for the count more than ten times with all his surgeries. Anyone with the strength to overcome what he overcame deserves so much. He has a sardonic, subversive wit, and he's really bright, but he's also fragile. It's difficult for him to get out on his own. Only now is he catching up for lost time. That's why I feel that we can never give him enough or indulge him enough. He doesn't understand the role

147

he plays in the family. He sees himself as the little brother, not someone whose strength has inspired us.

I really believe that I'm first and foremost a friend to my family and not someone who passes judgment on them. You can't be a friend if you're always judging, not a true friend. What I hope most is that I've brought them a sense of humour, but more important a flame that grows inside to want to change the status quo. All my kids want that. I believe a lot in sharing, and I think they've learned that from me. I always want to help someone in trouble. I spend more time worrying about my staff than myself. I always want to offer advice, or find a job for someone, or lend them a bit of money if they're going through a rough patch. Because I know what it's like to be down, and how important it is to have support to get you through it.

One of the things I talked about in my speech at Stacey's wedding is this whole notion of this roller coaster of life. There are so many people who are prepared to just sit in the station and never get on the ride and see it go up and up and up and then back to ground.

The strange part is that I didn't realize that at that time I was cresting the top of the roller coaster myself. The next month, in October 1993, Cott stock would hit $49⅝. In 1989 $100 invested in Cott was worth $14,000. Around that time the shorts entered the picture with a real passion, and the paranoia was full throttle. The market was starting to think that Coke had launched its counterattack. We hired David Goldman from Oppenheimer and Co. to head up investor relations, to keep interest high. By December it was trading at ninety times its twelve-month average earnings, while the TSE was trading at twenty-eight times.

While all that was going on, I went on an around-the-world trip with Nancy, and Dave and Terri Nichol. We travelled from Toronto to Sydney, to Melbourne, to Hong Kong, Johannesburg, Cape Town, Morocco to Venice. We stopped in Fiji for some R&R. We went to a resort called Wakaya owned by David Gilmour, Peter Munk's ex-partner. It's one of the most beautiful places I've ever seen. At mealtime a waiter would ask, "What kind of fish do you want?" And you'd say, "Red snapper." The next thing you'd see is some guy running into the ocean, throwing a spear, and then coming back with the fish.

Natives of Fiji don't drink alcohol. Instead they have a substitute called kava, made from the peppercorn plant. They make a big ritual out of it. They clap three times and they perform a ceremony every time you have a drink. One lunch we had began around one and ended about five. The kava ceremony was a dominant part of it. What we didn't realize was how potent this stuff was. It gives you rubber legs. And it started to rain heavily in the middle of this kava exercise and I didn't even get up. We couldn't get up. The rain was whipping around us, like a monsoon. And we couldn't move.

I don't remember asking Dave Nichol to work with me at Cott. In a way it was sort of destined. He travelled with me quite a bit before he left Loblaw, which they knew about, though not everyone there was happy about it. But it was never a secret from their people or ours. Nichol got me an enormous amount of free hype, talking with analysts, talking with newspapers, talking with customers. I didn't need him to talk to anybody on my behalf, ever. It was enough for him to talk about premium private label. All he had to talk about was President's Choice's 60 per cent penetration in the cola category. That's the best hype you can get—third party. He talked about the brand tax, and how consumers were sick and tired of paying it. And that's one of the reasons why I felt that I owed him. He was willing to put a private-label manufacturer at the forefront. He also gave me a whole bunch of ideas for new products over the years that allowed us to sell cola cheaper and cheaper.

There were rumours everywhere, started by the short sellers, no doubt, that I paid him off, which is complete nonsense. None of that has ever been substantiated and it never will be because it never happened! The rumours became so ridiculous that Nichol started joking publicly about me setting up a bank account for him in the Cayman Islands. People want to believe all of that kind of baloney when the fact was it was just a lot of good, hard work that made Cott a success.

By 1993 Dave had pretty much decided to leave Loblaw. He felt penned in and was really excited by what we could accomplish at Cott. He had even broached the subject with Galen Weston. They had been close friends since university. Galen didn't want to lose him. But there's no way Galen would have been willing to pay Dave a third of what I would pay him. I guess I raised the bidding war. I believed he was worth this money. That summer, Galen called me to his house. He lives a few blocks from me in Forest Hill. He asked me to leave Dave alone. But I couldn't. I couldn't break the loyalty for all Dave did for Cott. Even though I knew I was doing the wrong thing, I did it anyway. Nancy says that Evel Knievel was nothing compared to me.

Today, I look back on it as one of the biggest mistakes I've made. Why would I do that? Why would I do that to my biggest customer? Why? Why would I do it after Galen begged me not to? The only answer I can come up with is one that I'm not happy about. I have to think about it before I even can say it. And that is, it was self-destructive. I knew I was on the edge, had so much adrenaline pumping into me. I got into that spot with Galen because I created too much expectation in Nichol's mind and I couldn't get out of it. I realized I was wrong. I knew it was going to hurt my business, that it wasn't nice. It's not what I wanted to stand for. It was the imperfect side of me coming out. The kid part of me. Nichol was a trophy, and until I had the trophy I wasn't happy.

I was in a bind. If I turned Nichol back after that point, I'd have an enemy for life. I lost before I could win. I could have achieved the same thing without having annoyed Galen. To this day I'm sorry. I want to apologize to him.

In November Dave left Loblaw and became a consultant, doing a lot of work for us. He had his accountant sign up our deal while the guy was in the hospital about to undergo heart bypass surgery. The accountant was practically being wheeled into surgery but Nichol had to have the contract signed. That's an example of how aggressive he can be.

A few weeks later, USA Today called Cott "Big League Cross-Border Terrorists," featuring a picture of me with Dave and Don Watt. We were called the "trio leading the private label revolution from the no-frills, cheesy image of the 1970s." It went on to say that we were "setting up an assault on RJR Nabisco, Coca-Cola, and Anheuser-Busch." But by then our stock was beginning to slump. Talk about a roller coaster. When I started, the stock was at 31 cents. Five years later it was at $49.62. But by June 1994 it was trading around $19.50, thanks in part to the concerted effort of the shorts. But Coke and Pepsi were fighting back.

So what did I do? I raised the stakes. I figured that about 80 per cent of Coke's profits came from international operations. There was no reason we couldn't play on the same turf. We had formed Cott Europe at the end of 1993. Cadbury Schweppes had the use of the name Cott in United States from the time they'd bought out my dad's old partners, the Silver brothers. When we expanded into the U.S. they objected to the use of Cott's trade name. We responded by suggesting a joint venture. They decided to investigate and hired Monitor, a consulting company, which sent Simon Lester over to do some due diligence. Simon was no more than thirty. He comes across like the typical Brit, but he's a very smart, entrepreneurial guy. He worked for Cadbury Schweppes for a few years and then went to Monitor.

In the middle of this I got a telephone call from a senior executive at J. Sainsbury, which is the largest grocery chain in England, with more than four hundred stores. The managing director was in the United States and saw the great success of the Wal-Mart program. He got hold of us to see if we could help them to do the same thing in the U.K. It was a real coals-to-Newcastle situation. Private label was born there, thanks to Marks and Spencer, which had been a pioneer at the turn of the century. Penetration of private label in Europe had grown to over a third of grocery sales. But at Sainsbury they were never more than cheap fighter brands, even though they were 60 per cent of sales. I went to the U.K. We talked about what we could do to help them. It was the first time they had brought in an outside firm to do manufacturing, as far as I know.

In January 1994 we signed a deal with Cadbury Beverages to

produce the company's products across all Continental and Eastern Europe. Except, of course, in Great Britain, where Cadbury had a deal with Coke. That month we bought a 51 per cent stake in Benjamin Shaw, a small bottling company in Yorkshire. It was the largest independent bottler in the U.K. and supplied most of the supermarket trade. Once again we were starting from scratch. I hired Simon to help spearhead Europe. I made him a junior partner in the European business, which gave him enormous incentive to do well. He put that whole thing together over there, hiring another dozen people, and made it an enormous success.

We launched Sainsbury's Classic Cola in April 1994. Cola consumption is about 50 to 60 per cent in the U.K. to what it is here on a per capita basis, but it's still significant. At Sainsbury it was 25 pence a can. Coke cost 32 pence. We developed a five-and-a-half-ounce can that we gave away to get customers to try it. We had point-of-sale advertising that private labels never had before. We set up vending machines. It was the most successful launch, I think, in U.K. history.

The day after the launch Simon opened his *Times* of London. On page five he saw the headline "If anyone tells you their Cola's the same as Coke, don't buy it" with a picture of Sainsbury Cola under it. It was an ad by Coke, part of a $5 million campaign against us. They also used the slogan "Nothing else tastes like Coca-Cola" and "We only make the real thing." But it backfired on them by giving us enormous free hype. The publicity was unbelievable. It was discussed on breakfast television, evening television. The actress Carrie Fisher, a committed Coke drinker, appeared on Clive James as a "cola expert," took a blind taste test, and said ours was better than Coke. In two months, the Sainsbury cola captured 75 per cent of the store's cola sales, enough to account for 15 per cent of the U.K. market. Coke said that the packaging was too close to theirs and threatened to sue. We modified the packaging. By the first quarter of 1995, private label was 45 per cent of the U.K. cola market, double a year earlier.

News of the Sainsbury success spread. By July Simon had been called by every big supermarket chain in Europe. We were approached by Promodes, a huge French retailer with interests throughout Europe. Even retailers in Eastern Europe were calling. Many wanted exclusive relationships, which gave us some predictability.

◆ ◆ ◆

My son first came up with the idea of doing some kind of deal with Richard Branson, the founder of Virgin Group, which runs Virgin Records and Virgin Airlines. I didn't even know who he was. Clarke figured that he had different venues and he could possibly sell his own brand of cola on the airplanes. So we wrote to Branson directly about this opportunity, but I never heard back from him.

Nobody thought about it again until a guy named Ric Huning, a businessman in Wales, called Simon Lester. He had approached Virgin about doing a joint-venture cola deal. At this time Virgin was entering consumer products. It had its own vodka brand and was talking about doing a Virgin Mary pre-mix. Virgin shrugged Huning off, but that didn't deter him. He went out and got a trademark on "Virgin Cola" for the U.K., the U.S., Australia, and South Africa. Then he met with Simon to ask if we'd be interested in producing it. This was a coincidence, because Simon had the same idea for a while. After the meeting with Huning, Simon wrote directly to Branson to tell him. Now Branson wasn't about to get scooped out of his own deal. He was livid about it. Simon set up a meeting and went to see Branson with a prototype of a potential Virgin can, which the Watt Group designed and couriered overnight. And it turns out Branson was really interested. It was a great way to make it happen really fast. The next thing we know I'm invited to Branson's house on Necker, his island in the Virgin Islands. I took Clarke and Dave, because we wanted to pitch the prospect of a Virgin line of private-label food as well.

We took our plane to the Virgin Islands where Branson's helicopter met us. The first thing I saw in the cabin was Mick Jagger's autograph, scrawled like graffiti on the wall. The island was sensational, with beautiful white beaches. A truck met us and took us over gravel roads up a steep hill to the main house, which was beautifully done in the Balinese style. He brought carpenters at great cost to create a perfect copy of a Balinese house. It probably would have been easier for him to buy Bali. It's completely open, with no doors, no windows, but a great big thatched roof. Inside there are a number of very beautiful bedrooms. The baths and the showers were all outside, carved out of stone. They were filled with Body Shop products, which made sense when we found out Anita Roddick, the founder of the Body Shop, was coming with her family for a visit the next day. There were also too many salamanders. I put my hand down on one when I was turning on the water for my shower and got a little frightened.

It's a very special place. And he has the only snooker table in the islands. If the family isn't there, Branson rents the rooms out for some astronomical amount. When we arrived, Richard and his wife, Joan, and his kids, Sam and Holly, came up to meet us.

155

He was wearing this colourful muumuu thing, a sarong, and sandals. It was all very relaxed. We swam together and then ate outside sitting around this huge table. His other guests were the musician Peter Gabriel and his girlfriend. Clarke had to tell me who Peter was; I thought he was Branson's lawyer. They were playing a Peter Gabriel CD and it kept skipping. Clarke thought that was hilarious, that the guy who ran Virgin Records was listening to music that skipped. Branson also had a copy of *Naked Gun 33 &1/3*. He had done a deal with Blockbuster and here he had this pirated video.

We had an enjoyable evening together. I liked Richard immediately. He's soft, almost introverted, and he listens well. He's very tenacious and aggressive, even though everything that he does is very well thought through. He's a very down-to-earth kind of guy, very laid-back, not what you'd think of the typical Englishman. I didn't know much about his background other than he's considered one of the five or six most trusted names in England. We didn't negotiate, just talked about the opportunity and how I envisioned it. What struck me most was how fertile his mind was. We talked about the potential of going into other consumer products. I brought him some samples of some different products for him and his wife to try. That idea never went anywhere, maybe because he wanted to do it himself later. He wanted to limit it to drinks—cola and maybe bottled water.

Obviously his wife has been a big part of his success. She has given him the freedom he needs to grow. Joan was a topless model before they were married, and the *Sun* found out about it. A reporter phoned him and said, "Mr. Branson, I'd like you to know we found out that your wife was a topless model. And we want your comment." Now, what would the average guy say? "No comment." But Richard picked up the phone right away and joked about it. He turned the whole thing around. He's a genius. He's another guy who believes nothing is impossible. He's a rebel, and always full of play.

We stayed one night, and by the time we left, he wanted to create this Virgin Cola company. I went back to London and hammered out a deal with Trevor Abbott, the managing director of Virgin. Before he worked for Virgin, Trevor was an agent for Tom Jones and Englebert Humperdinck. He's as tough as nails, one of the smartest businessmen I've ever negotiated with. We went in as full partners. Cott put up half of all the capital plus the infrastructure to produce it. We immediately put a whole team of Retail Brands people from Toronto in London, including my daughter Holly and some of the best talent at the Watt Group. I spent a lot of time there as well. It was a real team effort. Branson had his own design people work on the final packaging. The actual cola formulation was done in Columbus by Prem Vermani.

We were really pumped up about it. At one of our meetings at Cott in June, somebody made a joke: "Oh, wouldn't it be great to say Virgin screws Coke."

Originally we were going to smaller stores and independents. Then Branson decided he wanted to go to a giant and he ended up with an exclusive deal at Tesco, which was the number-two supermarket chain in England. In the summer of 1993 they opened the product to general distribution. That concerned me because I didn't want to compromise our relationship with Sainsbury. That's why I stayed away from the marketing of Virgin Cola. I heard from the people at Sainsbury every day. They weren't too happy. It took Sainsbury a year and a half to get over it with us, even though they've remained a bigger seller than Virgin.

It would probably be fair to ask what we were even doing with Branson. It isn't our business. We're not a branded soft-drink company and he's a brand. Of course what makes him interesting is that he's a brand that crosses over a whole bunch of categories. I think the guy is nothing short of an absolute genius because there are very few brands in the world that carry from category to category—that are good for airlines, good for cola, good for record stores. He has a real lifestyle brand. That said, the Virgin deal is something I probably shouldn't have done. But we were looking for a critical production mass. But more than that I liked the romance of it. And I like Richard.

The Virgin launch started with big hype. I was amazed at how popular he is. We'd see kids in the street going up to him and saying "Hey, Richard." Despite the fact he's a multi-millionaire, he's perceived as this Robin Hood type, who's on the side of the little guy. From my personal experience with him I found that to be true. One night I went out for dinner with him at a Greek restaurant on Charlotte Street in London, with Simon, Clarke and Nik Kirkbride, the president of Virgin Cola Group. It was great fun. He told a great story about having a big dinner for the band Dire Straits, whom he was about to sign. He put out these Indian candies that looked like drugs on the tables. It turned out these guys were born-again, or anti-drug. They didn't under-stand and cancelled their contract.

Afterwards, he wanted everyone to go to this club called Beach Blanket Babylon. So we were all crammed into one of our little Mitsubishi trucks. Richard doesn't have a driver. So we're looking for the place and we're in a pretty seedy neighbourhood. Richard rolls down his window to ask a person living on the street for directions. And this guy says, "Aren't you Richard Branson?" He tried to help with directions but he didn't know where it was. Then he asks another street guy. This guy knew where it was. So what does he do as a way of saying thanks? He tells them both to get in the van. Instead of six of us, now there's eight of us. All night, Richard sat across from these guys and talked with them. He was picking their brains. He was curious about what kind of music they liked, their experiences on the street, how people think out there.

Around the time of his birthday one year he was in Toronto, so I took him to a pretty racy strip club on King Street. I go there once a year. I take my son-in-law there occasionally, for fun. So I take the world-famous Richard Branson, David, and Clarke.

The next day I went with him to the University of Manitoba, where he had been named the entrepreneur of the year. He had been up all day and night before and had two girls sitting on his lap for hours. All the students wanted to ask him questions. So he went to the local bar with a bunch of them and he stayed up until four or five o'clock in the morning talking to them about his philosophy.

Richard walks on the edge. I walk on the ledge. He's the greatest hypemeister in business today. There's no one more brilliant in promoting himself. He gets hundreds of millions of dollars a year for nothing. And that's his number-one way of building his brand. When we launched Virgin Cola in London on a very cold day, he got behind in this speedboat and he water-skied pulled by a blimp. And he went on two or three balloon rides. On one of them he was swept away and landed two thousand miles off course in the Arctic. People go crazy for this kind of stuff. Once he wanted to go around the world, so I lent him my airplane as a chase plane in case he went off course. He didn't have anything that small. He took off and landed in the desert somewhere.

He even wanted to take a can of air and sell that. His plan was to capture air when he went up in the balloon, and then sell it at like ten times the price of a soft drink. Brilliant. He also came up with the idea for Virgin Energy, a high-energy soft drink, containing caffeine, ginseng, and passion fruit. When he launched it in May 1995, outside the Swallow Hotel in London, he stopped traffic. He handed out free condoms with tins of the drink and press packs. Richard stripped down to his t-shirt and yellow boxer shorts with a happy face on them and jumped into a thirty-foot mobile bed with Pamela Anderson Lee, that blonde with the silicon boobs from *Baywatch*. What Richard didn't know was that there was a gap in his shorts for the world to see. He ended up covering it with a baseball hat. The guy never pays for publicity. Talk about hype. He's got millions and millions of dollars of free publicity.

We haven't kept in touch. I talked to him just before I got sick about a customer that he wanted to make an investment in. I could have built on the Virgin franchise, but that was around the time things at the company were becoming a little tough for me. I was busy trying to get my arms around it all.

One of the great triumphs for me was getting to speak several times at Harvard Business School. In 1993 Harvard Business School did a study of Cott. Before that they had done studies of Loblaw and the Watt Group. I gave a couple of addresses. One was to the M.B.A. class and one to the managers. It was an important moment for me. My brother Bill graduated from Harvard, but my M.B.A. came from real life. I don't know the first thing about management theory.

The students loved me. They had never seen a real down-to-earth guy. The first thing I said to them was that I had only graduated from high school and that standing there in front of them was the biggest thrill I could have. They voted me the best case study. The next year they wrote up another one about our business with Virgin.

Rules of Business

I have a little card that I hand out to my people, which talks about the values of the company. And the values are very simple.

Number one, you have to respect the people who work with you—not only co-workers but customers and suppliers.

The second thing that I think is very important is intensity. People have to be willing to make the sacrifices that are required to run a business as intensely as it needs to be run and as if it was their own.

Number three is the whole idea of creating interdependence with various stakeholders.

And last but not least is the ability to share not only financially but also in all the good things and the bad things that happen to a business. You can't take all the accolades and not be willing to take credit for the errors or failures. A lot of people do that. If you want to share, share in the whole thing.

I never go to charitable events, never to industry affairs, nothing. I have so many things to do that when I have time, I stay home. We decided at one point not to become active again in the Canadian Soft Drink Association because it's controlled by Coke and Pepsi.

The days of taking people for a golf game and for dinners and a $50,000 Château Whatever are over. People now want information, they want knowledge, they want respect, they don't want to be patronized. They want to learn.

But with my suppliers I've never been an entertainer. I don't drink—I don't enjoy that and most people do. And I would try my best if possible to have people who worked for the company in very senior jobs look after that side of the relationship with suppliers and customers. I never go out to lunch, so I never obviously take customers to lunch. But I always know what was important and have to work that much harder because the old sense of selling is long gone and won't ever be back.

The game is changing in supermarkets. There are no more promotional coupons, no stamps—they have to produce better pricing. People are corrupt everywhere, but that's changing because of technology. They used to give you an order by hand, and now it's all recorded. It's not the same game any more. So if you want to play Machiavellian games, play big ones. The old-time food brokers who show up with a bag of money are dead.

I never was the guy with the fancy Christmas baskets. I never sent anything to any customer. But give me the opportunity to help somebody who is sick or help somebody find a job, and I'm always there. It's not unethical to phone a customer whose wife is sick and ask him how she is. And yet how many people would take the time to do that? Between slim and none, because everybody has got too much going on to remember little things.

◆ ◆ ◆

By 1994 I was under pressure. One minute the stock was trading just under $18. A few weeks later it was $13 and change. The short position was something like nearly nine million shares. What vultures.

I named Dave Nichol president of Cott in September 1994, the same time Virgin Cola was launched. Until then he had been consulting to us. By then the relationship with Heather had run dry. She wanted to be chief operating officer of the business, but I wasn't prepared to let her do that. I didn't feel that was where her strengths were. She had the title of president and I was never going to take it away from her, but I was never going to let her run the company. That really rankled her. For a long time, she had my ear full-time. Then I brought in Danny Silver and Dave, and she wasn't too happy about that. I thought Danny would be a great officer at Cott to deal with personality conflicts. He's a great filter and buffer. Every company should have its own shrink.

I guess she saw them as threatening. She didn't want Danny there, and she didn't want Nichol there. Things clearly were not working out between us, and after I appointed Dave president, she left.

Bringing Nichol into such a prominent position created very strained, big emotions with Loblaw in the beginning. They would have loved to throw Cott out, I'm sure, if they had a viable alternative. We kept the accounts for the soft drinks, the bottled water, the pet food, the snacks. All of it. It would have been foolish for them to drop us. No one could match us. But the store reduced our shelf space and promotion in favour of Coke and Pepsi, who offered big price reductions and deal-backs, so it was profitable to them again. We lost the contract with Loblaw to produce PC beer, though. They took it to Labatt. I have to admit, I got outsmarted at Lakeport. We bought the brewery for nothing and suddenly we had $20 million of value. Then, virtually the next day, it had no value because Galen sold the rights to Labatt. They paid $40 million for the rights, four times what it was worth. I can't blame Galen for taking it.

But things have been smoothed out. We have a better relationship now than we've ever had with them. Now it's down to a level of business.

Dave and I didn't always agree on what his priorities should be. I wanted him to help Cott with marketing and to give Cott a competitive advantage. I needed him to come up with new categories to Cott-icize. But he was interested in developing products, through Destination Products International, which Cott owned 85 per cent of. Dave owned the rest. What I needed was new soft drinks, but he was interested in producing the next Memories of Beirut. I thought that here was this marketing genius who could figure out how to keep adding more value to our customers. I thought he would open doors and he did. He was okay with a couple of customers. Dave had great bravado but was shy with customers without me. He couldn't yell at them. Maybe it was my mistake to think that other retailers would listen to him. He tended to focus on criticizing their operations, which is not the way to make a deal happen. But the biggest problem with bringing Dave in was that it took my eye off dealing with everyday values that I believed in. That was the price of buying a megastar.

◆ ◆ ◆

In May 1995, Gerry Schwartz called me to his office. He told me I was off the Onex board. He said I had missed three meetings and that he felt I had too much to do. I was shocked. I was his best friend for a long time and I would say, if he looks in his heart, he would still probably say that was true of me. Schwartz and I would do deals on the back of an envelope that involved millions of dollars. That's how much trust there was between us. I didn't say anything when he was telling me this, I was so hurt. I just ate it. I very much regretted having to do that. It hurt me more than anything in my career.

I was there in the beginning for him, and today he runs the fourth-biggest or fifth-biggest company in Canada. I was his largest investor in his first public issue. And I think at one stage I was the largest shareholder in his business. In 1984 Financial Trustco invested $2.8 million in Onex. By 1987 we had almost 12 per cent of the company, which was worth something like $50 million to us. I helped him to capitalize the business. I was involved in staffing, I was on the executive committee, and was instrumental in big decisions. We also had made some great investments over the years. We're both investors in Vincor, the largest wine company in Canada. It's a fantastic business—it's done very, very well. We went public in June 1996. For every dollar I put in, I've returned seven or eight. I did very well. We also bought KIK, which is the largest private-label bleach manufacturer in North America, in 1991. My son-in-law, David, started running it in January 1995 and he's doing a brilliant job. Its revenues are over $100 million.

But more than any of our business dealings, I was the guy Schwartz leaned on when he needed to lean on somebody's shoulder. I helped him through some difficult times. As he supported me. He was really supportive after Financial Trustco ran into trouble. When it bombed I had to liquidate my Onex shares. I stayed on his board, stayed on his executive committee, stayed on his audit committee. He never gave up his support for me. He was a big investor in Cott in the early days. I don't know exactly how much he made on Cott, but I've been told it's over $50 million. Schwartz may have more money than I do, but I've had a lot more fun. So have the people around me. That's what turns me on.

I have lots of good memories of our relationship. About two years after I went to work at Cott, after the PC Cola took off, he and Heather hosted a black-tie dinner with all the people who had stood by me over the years. They invited Fraser Latta, Larry Tanenbaum, Larry Shapiro, Steve Halperin, Danny Silver, Lawrence Bloomberg, Dan Casey, and Brian Foley, who's with Coopers and Lybrand, and, of course, Nancy. They even designed a can of pop with the guest list on it.

The whole thing with Heather was ugly and a lot of it is my own fault. You can't win when you bring your best friend's wife into that kind of role. I wasn't too smart. I realize now that the way I brought in Dave wasn't nice for her. I could have been more thoughtful. I figured this was a good opportunity. So she was gone and he was in. That's what happened. And then she was so devastated by it all.

We did all kinds of things together over the years. And he was a guy that I really had fun with. We've had such wonderful vacations together. Once, about 1984, Clarke was recovering from a surgery. Schwartz helped me arrange a holiday at the Hôtel du Cap in the south of France for a week. I took Nancy, Clarke, and a friend of his. Schwartz told me about this restaurant across the way from the Hôtel du Cap that has fantastic onion rings and lobster. He went on and on about how I had to go there. So we get to the Hôtel du Cap and it's a very nice place, and we go to the restaurant and eat. Afterwards, they gave us a wonderful boat tour. Then comes the bill: $37,000 U.S. for a week. So the first thing I look for is where is the $15,000 deposit I gave them. They told me that's already included. I asked them how this could have happened. They said, "Well, we told Mr. Schwartz we could only rent during that time eight days in a row. And since you could only come for six, you have to pay the other two." Then I looked at the lunch bill and found out it was something like $3,000 for the four of us to have this lobster dinner, including the boat to and from the hotel. Then there was the room service Clarke and his friend had. So finally we figured it all out, and I went to pay it. Then I found they don't accept credit cards. So I had to sit in the middle of Cap d' Antibes, at the American Express branch, trying to get enough money on my American Express card to pay. Schwartz just laughed when I told him about it.

Halfway through 1995 I realized that things had to change. We had just signed a bunch of new accounts—Stop 'N Shop and Kmart in the U.S., Hakon in Norway, Greenberg Stores in Israel, the Hero Group in Indonesia. We bought a spring-water bottling company in the U.K. and signed Virgin Cola in Ireland and Japan. We were doing spring water and high-intensity beverages for Wal-Mart. We bought the remainder of the Watt Group. We were doing soft drinks for Safeway and Woolworth in the United Kingdom, which gave us nearly a quarter of the U.K. market.

The top line was growing but the bottom line wasn't keeping up. The company had grown so fast in such a short period of time without a solid foundation. We had no infrastructure to serve new clients or to be a low-cost provider. What's the use of producing for some guy in Charlotte, North Carolina, if you've got to spend more money to get it there? We veered away from premium brands and did some cheaper generics that compete with the premium brands.

This voice in my head was shouting: "Focus, Gerry, focus!" We grew this business internally without acquisition from a point that the company had $30 million of sales to the point that we've got about a $1.2 billion. It's my strength and weakness that I can't say no. I've had retailers from all over the world phoning me every day. I found it very hard to get a call from one of the biggest retailers in Spain and turn him down.

But we got to a point that the more business we did, the more it cost, and we weren't getting any leverage out of it, and that was showing on our bottom line. And so I realized that two things had to happen if the company was going to survive and prosper long term. One, it needed to have some time to breathe. We had to put in the infrastructure that it needed to run the business properly. At the same time, it had to catch its breath and not grow all over the place, and it had to realize that it can't be in every business at the same time.

My dad wasn't a disciplined guy. I'm not a disciplined guy. But my lack of discipline has worked for me because I've been able to harness it and use it to my advantage. This little thing, Cott, took over the United States. If I was disciplined I couldn't do that. I would have been more worried about all the implications of these decisions that I was making. Becoming the General Foods of private label was a great dream, but I've learned that you only need to be successful at executing one idea. And a lot of our ideas had become weight. We were left with a brewery with virtually no business. We faced losing our investment and having to close the place down, which would have put people out of work. We had to stop trying to double sales and be happy with 15 per cent. We had to concentrate. We put the kibosh on going into France, Germany, and Thailand as we had planned. We needed to focus on becoming a manufacturing company. We needed to become a much more efficient service organization. We needed to become a cheaper cost manufacturer. We needed to buy and build bottling plants.

I had two choices. Was I going to sit on the side and let someone else run this company? Or was I was going to take another challenge and learn to run it myself? I decided to do something I had never done before: become a manager. And that has been my priority for the past two years. It's a lot different from being an entrepreneur who creates. A manager takes the creation and maintains and builds on it. By this time the stock was trading around $8, but I wasn't worried about that. There comes a time when you've just got to forget about the stock market. You've got to run the business.

Don't get me wrong. I believe it's enough to create. The greatest builders in the world are entrepreneurs, not managers. God is an entrepreneur. Even leaders of the church are entrepreneurs. I heard Rev. Schuyler interviewed on *Larry King*. He was asked how he would describe himself. He said, a businessman.

I brought in Sandy Aird, the chairman of Deloitte & Touche's consulting business. He was really useful in helping me think through things. I also brought in True Knowles as a consultant. True used to be president of Dr Pepper Co. He's like the elder statesman of the beverage industry. Everyone respects him. He lives in Turtle Creek, near Dallas. When Cadbury Schweppes bought Dr Pepper, he was bought out. I hired a headhunter, who approached him. He didn't need to work and was resistant to the idea at first. After meeting with me, though, he signed on. I gave him stock options. True is much more methodical than I am. He makes sure there's water in the pool before he jumps in.

In November 1995 we made an announcement to the press. We said that there was a limit to how much a company could digest and that we had indigestion. We explained we were laying off employees, taking a $40-million writedown, and selling interests in non-core businesses to focus on core business. We scaled back. We got out of South Africa. The only reason we got in there is because Coke has a strong presence. We were partially successful but we didn't keep our eye on the ball. Logistics were a big problem, given the distance between Cape Town, Durban, and Johannesburg. With only one facility we couldn't make it work because of the transport costs. We still have a joint venture over there but we closed our plant. We lost quite a bit. We sold Murphy's Potato Chips, which Heather had advised me to buy, and part of our interest in Virgin. And at first we were partners with Branson for the world. We decided that it was too risky to do, and fighting Coke and Pepsi required too much money. Besides, it was Virgin who would get the benefit, even though we were paying half of that. So we decided to keep the U.K. business and basically we took a carried interest in the rest of the world in exchange for the interest that we had. Molson bought Lakeport from us. We invested $20 million and we were able to get $20 million out of it. So I went to Dave and asked him if he'd let me use his name and let Molson take over the Dave Nichol Selection beers. He agreed because he loved to get his mug on TV.

At the end of 1996 I assumed the role of president from Dave. I'm a very loyal guy, very, and he's given me a lot of good things for not only Cott but for this industry, and I don't forget. But you reach a point that you kind of lose the tips of your shoes because you've just been stepped on once too often.

I liked the idea of this challenge of doing something that I'd never done before. I was rolling up my sleeves and actually running the business. For once I would forget about getting the orders and figure out how to make the deliveries more profitable.

There's one point that I agree with Dave Nichol on, it's only a matter of time until retailer-controlled brands will have 30 to 40 per cent of the supermarket business in North America. Safeway has 30 per cent of its business in private label. There's consolidation going on in the supermarket industry. It's only a matter of time until people who run poor businesses for the most part will be gone.

I changed my attitude toward Coke and Pepsi. I stopped seeing them as our competitors. There is no more war. No more fight. We don't want to be the third-largest soft-drink company in the world. We want to be number one at controlling every case in the specialty segment. We want to own it, want to put everybody else out of business. And so I now have bent it to a point that I'm saying, Look, now I'm going to get Coke and Pepsi to get along with me. If we can consolidate the independent bottling capacity in the industry, it's going to be a $5 billion to $10 billion company. That's why Cott is going to have another amazing renaissance, because we're going to be the only one left. It's going to be us, Coke, and Pepsi. Nice business. That's why Cott is a company that doesn't have its future behind it.

I figured I was in a new round. Everything was going along, the way life does in between crises. The restructuring was going well. Cott seemed to have hit some kind of equilibrium. In the spring of 1997 I bought my first dog, Sophie, a beautiful Portuguese water dog. I threw a thirtieth wedding anniversary surprise party for Nancy in New York. But on May 20, 1997, everything turned around for me again. That was the day my tumor was diagnosed. And I was off on the biggest ride of all.

The Fight of My Life

The week between the diagnosis and the surgery on May 29 was intense. The weekend was a blur. Our family is emotional and close, even when things are going well, so you have to imagine this scene. At that point I hadn't been handed the dire statistics about life expectancy, though I had prepared myself for the fact that the tumor was malignant. I also had to face the fact that I might not make it through the surgery.

There was so much to do in terms of getting my business and personal affairs in order. I had never planned succession. I had always assumed I was invincible. So I called a meeting of Cott's senior management at my house for first thing Saturday morning. Humberto Aquino, Fraser Latta, my brothers-in-law Steve and Mark Halperin, my son-in-law, David, Mark Benadiba, and Sandy Aird were all there.

A sense of shock hung over everything. Everyone was concerned about my health and how I was dealing with it. Then we started focusing on the business. What struck me most was their faces. It was evident a new era had come for Cott. We had to be hard, practical. We divided the group into two segments—one dealt with the outside world, the other with interim internal planning. My brother-in-law Steve had my power of attorney. True Knowles was appointed the head of the executive management committee.

Danny Silver's daughter Carolyn got married that weekend and at the last minute I decided I should go. I figure that even though I've been given this life sentence, I wasn't going to sit around and mope. Very few people there knew about my tumor that night. Of course Danny knew, but I thought it was important for him that I went.

The days leading up to the surgery were a blur too. I had a succession of meetings about the business. The house was filled with people and food. My brothers arrived. Larry Shapiro and his wife flew in from Calgary. Larry has always been there for me. He was with us when Clarke had his surgery at the Mayo Clinic. There were a lot of tears but there was also a lot of laughter and food. My barber came over to shave my head. It was a major event; everyone crammed around and we videotaped it.

The strangest part was that for the first time in my life I liked the way I looked. I went upstairs and tried on some clothes I had bought at Bijan in New York a few months earlier, when Nancy and I had gone for our thirtieth wedding anniversary. On that visit I was walking down Madison Avenue and I saw a hat in the window that I thought Nancy would like. I bought the hat, then asked the saleslady if she could custom-make a couple of hats for me. I've never worn hats, partly because my head is so big that they don't usually fit. It seems strange now. Then I had no idea that this would happen to me and that maybe I would need to wear a hat.

Then I went into the Bijan store in the St. Regis Hotel where we were staying. I was cold and needed a sweater. I ended up spending about $100,000 in about two hours. I bought a couple of dozen shirts, a tuxedo, and a couple of cashmere coats. It was totally out of character for me to do that. I'm the kind of guy who's bought two suits a year for the past twenty years because of my yo-yo weight situation. But I really enjoyed buying this stuff. I was a little slimmer, thanks to my trainer,

Charlie, and I looked better in the clothes. They liked me so much at Bijan that they put a clock on the wall with my name on it. They have all their hundred best customers from around the world and clocks set in the time zone that they live in. So my clock is right under King Hussein's. Now I've got all this stuff, and I'll probably never wear it.

The night before the surgery, Stacey gave me a red thread to tie around my right ankle, called a *bendel*. Red is a lucky colour in the Jewish faith. A friend of hers brought it back from Israel, where it had been blessed by a rabbi. She put one on her ankle as well. I'm supposed to wear it until it falls off. She made everyone kiss this thing. Stacey has the heart of a tiger. Like me, she can be a little stubborn, but she has a fierce devotion. That was a sight. There was my brother Bill, who's not the most effusive guy in the world, kissing this piece of string. Bill isn't easy with his emotions. But it was supposed to bring good luck and I needed all the luck I could get.

Just before the surgery, Bill told me I was his hero. That meant more to me than anything. All my life I never felt I had his acceptance. He's been one of the demons motivating me, pushing me to prove myself, to gain his respect. It's never been his fault. It's my demon. I created it. And it's been with me for the past forty years. Hearing him say that meant more than anything.

The few first nights after the surgery I lay awake thinking about the changes going on inside my head. It wasn't the disease I was seeking out. I started thinking of my thoughts as if they were endangered species. Capturing them became important.

There's no kidding myself about the surgery solving the problem. The surgery only buys time before the tumor grows again. Dr. Bernstein told us it's next to impossible to remove all the microscopic tentacles attached to the tumor. They're like the roots of a plant and can regenerate the tumor all over again. He explained that my brain becomes the tumor, and the tumor wants to grow. It's very entrepreneurial.

I set up a meeting with Michael Levine for advice about my book. He's an entertainment and publishing deal maker who's a law partner of Steve Halperin's. He knows everybody. I want this book to reach a lot of people. Michael was very encouraging. He even talked about some interest from Canadian TV to do a documentary.

I've learned it's surprising what you're prepared to live with one day and what you're prepared to live with the next. In my case I would have thought that if I ever got something like this, I'm hiring Dr. Kevorkian. I'm giving him the job first.

My big fear is losing control. I'd control my family and my business from my grave, if I could. But my first lesson after diagnosis was that we have some inner guts that in inexplicable ways rise to the occasion. When I heard the diagnosis, I did what I always do. I looked for the opportunity in it. The first thing I realized was that this was a message to change my act. If it hadn't happened, I'd probably have run the day-to-day at Cott fifteen hours a day for the next fifteen years, even though I was becoming bored with it. Running a business growing at 10 to 15 per cent a year is not the kind of thing that turns me on. I know I couldn't make the same contributions in the second ten years of my life at Cott that I did in the first ten.

The greatest challenge at Cott was reinventing it. That's what created $3 billion of market value. I needed to prove to myself that I was capable of being a manager. That gave me inner satisfaction. Well, a year and a half it lasted and I did a pretty good job. But it would have been a waste of my time to continue. And that's what I would have done if I hadn't got this thing in my head. This tumor is the escape path God gave me so I don't have to do that any more. I guess it means I don't have to give a damn about a lot of things that preyed on me. It took a sledgehammer to make me understand that. A heart attack wouldn't have stopped me. Well, maybe for a month or six weeks. But then I'd have been back at it.

I'm in a tough mess. But if my life has taught me anything, I seem to be at my best in a mess. I believe the only way you get where you want to be is to never give up. That's how I've lived my life and that's how I'm going to fight this disease. Nothing is impossible, including beating a death sentence the way I have.

The first thing I did after Dr. Bernstein gave me my sentence was to figure out how the diagnosis didn't apply to me. I wondered if other people diagnosed are in as good condition as I'm in. I also figured that a lot of people just lie down and die because they can't cope. They don't have the alternatives available that I do. They can't work. They don't have any money. They can't get the right medical care. The other thing is that most people accept their fate. I've never been one to take no for an answer. Then I wondered how well they keep track of all these people after diagnosis. It occurred to me that people who have just been given a life sentence probably didn't rank too high on the medical establishment's priority list. And that's when I started to think about what I could do to change that.

I had to become my own doctor. That was the only way I could overcome the failure mentality that surrounded my disease. I knew I had to go out and search for the best treatment. I wasn't about to accept the status quo. I approached it the way I'd do a business deal. I'd question everything. And I'd create interdependency with my doctors. I needed to surround myself with the best team if I was going to have a chance. I bought my surgeon Mark Bernstein a great pen set, inscribed "To Dr. Markie from GBM Number One," GBM for glioblastoma multiforme. It's important to me that I not be just a statistic to him.

I've learned the importance of charming people who can save your life. When Nancy and I travelled to Europe in 1993 with Dave and Terri we went to Troisgros, in Rouen, France, a three-star restaurant, and one of the best in the world. Nancy cried, the food was so good. But I had excruciating stomach pain and didn't enjoy one bite. Afterwards we had to call a doctor. I thought I was dying. The next day, Dave, Terri, and Nancy went to another great restaurant for lunch, while I ended up in the local hospital. I asked the staff if they'd been to Troisgros. They hadn't. I told them that if they could make me better, I would send them. It turned out I had a kidney stone. They had to give me morphine, I was in so much pain. But I was true to my promise. Soon I treated nine of them to dinner with their husbands and wives. They sent a photograph of themselves toasting me.

It took me a while to get answers from my doctors—my surgeon, the oncologist, the radiation guy. It is even harder to talk them into deviating from their standard protocol. Every answer for everything seems to be "We don't know." I don't want to be in the last group of "we don't knows" who died when next year there's going to be something for them that could have been tested on me.

It's frustrating to stay optimistic, hearing everyone say, "Well, you do have a terminal illness." Everybody has a terminal illness.

The only difference is that mine has been diagnosed. It's ironic. They tell you, number one, you have a terminal disease. Then, number two, you have less than a year or two years to live. Then, number three, you'll take everything that the failed cases took. You end up getting what everyone else is failing on. It's not terribly encouraging. I want to break that mould.

I'm not exactly a willing patient. When I was thirty-five, I had my gall bladder removed. I had surgery on a Wednesday morning at ten o'clock. By the next night I was threatening the nurses that I wanted to go home. So the next morning I just walked out. I was in the hospital under forty-eight hours. I called a cab to take me home. You should have seen the look on Nancy's face when she opened the door. "Pay the cab, please," I told her as I walked into the house. "I'm home."

Most people do exactly what the doctor tells them. Take this pill. Do that. What I've learned here is that you better not trust anybody because you'll be following somebody's protocol and they don't want to screw up their research with one life.

The Wednesday after my surgery I went to Memorial Sloan-Kettering Hospital in New York with Nancy, my son-in-law, and Danny Silver. The news of my illness got around quickly after being announced on the Bloomberg terminal. Donald Drapkin, who works with Ron Perelman, had set up the visit. I had just seen Ron at Drapkin's daughter's bat mitzvah in New York about two weeks before my diagnosis. He was there with Penny Marshall, the film director. I met Ron years ago at a Drexel Burnham bond conference in 1983, long before he owned Revlon. He was buying a company called Pantry Pride. He already owned a company called MacAndrews and Forbes Holdings, which made chocolate and licorice extract. Licorice's number-one usage is in cigarettes. It adds flavour. Now

MacAndrews and Forbes is his holding company. Drapkin is the vice-chairman. He used to be one of the leading takeover lawyers on Wall Street. Ron is a very nice man. He's donated so much to medical research that I think he has a wing at Sloan-Kettering named after him. After they heard about my illness, they phoned to see if they could do anything to help me, which I really appreciated. At Revlon they have a full-time medical consultant, Dr. Robert Krasner, who has tremendous relationships with any hospital in America. That's the advantage of having connections.

I immediately got an appointment with Jerome Posner, the leading oncologist in the area. When we met I cross-examined him about the disease. I wanted to know what to expect. What happened in these cases? What were the odds of my having a stroke? Would I be in a coma? What was the risk of paralysis? How long did his other patients live with the same thing that I have? My thinking is that if I know what I'm up against—everything, no whitewashing—we could begin to find a way to beat it.

Posner basically agreed with the diagnosis. He told me that some of his patients live five to six years. Others died in a few months. It was really hard on Nancy to listen to it. We've been through tough times, but we've always survived. They also were positive about the quality of care I was getting in Toronto. Dr. Posner suggested I get a PET (positron emission tomography) scan, during which they insert this nuclear isotope to look for activity in the tumors. They inject dye, and if there is any activity in any tumor in the brain, it reveals it. There's one PET scanner in Toronto but it would have taken weeks to get an appointment. The scan showed no new activity in the tumor site but it showed the presence of other tumors, which depressed me a bit.

After the appointment, I took Nancy, Danny, and David for lunch at the Second Avenue Deli and had a feast. Here's a partial list of what we ate: chopped liver, kishka, meatballs, stuffed cabbage, pastrami, corned beef, two orders of fries, boiled beef, kasha and bow ties, chocolate cake, more cake, coffee.

It was great. I've never been one for fancy stuff. I get more pleasure eating the world's greatest hamburger than eating pâté de foie gras in the great restaurants of the world. We had to put three tables together to hold it all. The only one who could have eaten more was me. The bill came to $100. The waiter almost passed out when I gave him a $100 tip.

It was a relief to get back to Toronto. My beautiful grandson, Jesse, kissed me one thousand times. That night I had my first decent sleep since the surgery.

Then I met with Dr. Laperierre, the head radiologist at Princess Margaret, the leading Toronto centre for treating cancer, to discuss radiation therapy. He floored me with more statistics that really depressed me. I cried. Radiation is supposed to double life expectancy. If you had six months to live, radiation should extend it to a year. The downside is terrible side effects like nausea and fatigue. There's also the risk that you can lose around ten IQ points. That isn't a big concern; I'm more worried about losing my appetite. I also met with Warren Mason, a neuro-oncologist at Toronto Western Hospital. He's a young guy, in his early thirties, but he's one of the best in Canada. He's one of Posner's protégés. He studied with him in New York.

Deciding on a course of action is difficult. There's a lot of debate about what works and what doesn't. Nancy and I are reading everything we can about clinical trials. The other thing we did was look for sites on brain tumors on the Internet. There are a bunch of them: Massachusetts General Hospital, Harvard Medical School, University of Texas's M.D. Anderson Center.

The facts are pretty sobering. Malignant brain tumors are only a little more than 1 per cent of all cancers diagnosed, but they add up to 2.4 per cent of deaths due to cancer. Brain tumors are the second leading cause of death among children under nineteen, and the third leading cause among adults under forty. The incidence of brain tumors is increasing, and nobody knows why. There was quite a lot that was positive, though. You'd hear about people who live twelve years. The most impressive thing we read was by a young guy named Steve DePesa who lives in California. He was diagnosed with a GBM, the same tumor as mine, in March 1996 but he's doing great. No symptoms. He put together a summary of what to expect. Nancy started e-mailing him, and we're helping him to publish his report to the general public.

What I found out was that 90 per cent of the test group just drop off the radar. You don't know what their fate was. So I kind of reversed it and said we want to understand more about the 90 per cent and how many of those people could have done better and lived longer if they had the opportunity. That's when the idea of setting up a foundation to deal with brain tumors came to me. It was a quick decision. But it felt right. I sit on the boards of Toronto's Mount Sinai Hospital, the B'nai B'rith Foundation, and the Weitzman Institute of Canada. I also used to sit on the board of Toronto's Clarke Institute Foundation for psychiatric research and the Hebrew University in Jerusalem. I've given away a lot of money, millions. Nancy and I set up a foundation, and over the years we've supported the State of Israel Bond program, the United Jewish Appeal, the Israel Children's Tennis Centers, Ontario College of Art, and

Toronto's Design Exchange. A few years ago, we gave money to the Mount Sinai Hospital to set up an endoscopy unit for colon cancer and inflammatory bowel disease. But all the time I just wrote the cheque. I was never really involved with it. I never touched it. I never felt it do any good for anyone. I want this to be the best-funded centre of its kind. I don't like half measures. My career has been built around being an innovator, never giving up, making things happen, being a catalyst for change, a change maker. I want to bring that to the foundation. The private sector is having to fund everything. It's having to come to the rescue of educational institutions, all of the horrible gaping holes in the system.

My approach has always been to turn a negative into a positive. The whole thing together is too overwhelming, but piece by piece you can deal with it. I'm not looking here to just hit some more home runs. I've made more than enough money. Even if my stock went down 80 per cent, I'd still be rich. And that's why I'm so convinced that I want to make a difference to people. You give 10 per cent in one shot of everything you have. Maybe I can give more, I don't know.

I'm trying to learn to take one day at a time. I'm surprised by how much I like being at home, away from the office. Never, ever did I go anywhere without phoning the office at least three times a day.

I have two assistants who work out of my house—Linda McKie and Joan Burns. I need them both because even though I'm not going into the office every day, my schedule hasn't slowed down at all.

I feel so much seems possible. I'm about to fly through another window. The tumors they found at Sloan-Kettering were benign, which was great news, but their presence meant that I wasn't eligible for gene therapy.

I feel confident I'm creating a great team to help me. Charlie, my trainer, has been really useful in discussing steroids with my doctors. Steroids can control the swelling, or edema, created by brain tumors. Charlie has great questions. He knows as much about this stuff as they do. Actually he probably knows more.

◆ ◆ ◆

Having wonderful parties has been a big part of my family's life. There have been so many that I can't remember them all. A few years ago Nancy and I got remarried on the island of Anguilla for our twenty-fifth anniversary. It was a huge surprise. All I told Nancy before leaving was that she needed a white dress. I arranged to have the kids meet us on the beach, all dressed up. I hired Rabbi Schecter, our family's rabbi during the Calgary years, to remarry us. I wore a tuxedo with the pants cut off at the knees so we could wade into the water together to be photographed against the sunset. Nancy was so thrilled with the surprise that she couldn't stop crying with joy.

Just after I embarked on the restructuring at Cott I wanted to have a fiftieth birthday for her and hire the Beach Boys to play. I also had this big party planned this summer for our thirtieth wedding anniversary in the country. I rented the *Seguin*, that big boat in the Muskokas, where we have our cottage, for the whole weekend. We cancelled that also three weeks before I knew I was sick. It just didn't feel right.

The day after we got back from Sloan-Kettering, we had a

party for Stacey's and Jesse's birthday. The next day was Clarke's twenty-fourth birthday. We shopped together and bought him a beautiful Zenith metallic blue Porsche Boxster. I wanted to him to have freedom and more self-confidence. It gives me such pleasure to see him this excited. One benefit of being home is that I get to spend a lot of time with him.

A few days after Clarke's birthday, Holly threw a party for me at the office. Holly has Nancy's sense of style. Even with all this stuff in my head I was very excited by it. I gave a little speech about being hit by four lightning bolts in one life. This was just one more hurdle. I will make it. I believe that. I want to believe that.

All the directors came, except Dave Nichol. He has tremendous pressure on him right now. His business isn't doing well and we're trying to figure out what we should do with it. But I also think he's having a difficult time dealing with my illness. I spent the rest of the day at Cott. But I have to admit I didn't like it. Ten years at Cott, I loved every minute.

I'm a little weaker. The adrenaline kick that came with my diagnosis is wearing off. I know I can't keep up this pace. I have to conserve strength for the radiation program I'm beginning at Princess Margaret Hospital. I'm taking the highest possible dose. It's a five-week cycle, five days a week, thirty seconds a session. They fit you with a helmet that looks like the face mask the goalie Jacques Plante used to wear. Then you're bolted to the table. They slide you into the machine. It's claustrophobic. It's more frightening than my operation. You can't speak. You can't move. It lasts two minutes, and you don't feel anything. It's the anguish that's in your mind that you're really feeling. It's something that I'd like to get behind me.

I'm finding that some of my reactions to things surprise me.

The other day Clarke and Holly were joking around with me in my office at Cott before a board meeting. My brother-in-law Mark Halperin, our corporate secretary, came into my office and asked, "Should we start the board meeting without you?" I went ballistic. Maybe it's my own insecurity. The board meeting went well. Earnings are up 50 per cent. The stock is flying; it's at a twelve-month high.

The next day I was off to New York to meet with analysts. I led the meeting, which felt good. Then we went to Morgan Stanley to talk about different options for the company. I see myself in a new phase now. So I'm debating whether the family should keep its 29 per cent stake in Cott. It's been a heart-wrenching decision. There's so much involved. I believe that my kids have to find their own way. My wife needs security, but how much is enough? Afterwards, we hit the Carnegie Deli. I even went to Bijan to buy more clothes. We went for a late dinner to Peter Luger in Brooklyn for steak. The place was so crowded that I had to tell the maître d' I had a brain tumor to get a table.

The days are flying by. I'm finding my writing is getting worse and worse. Father's Day was on Sunday. It was very emotional for me. My son-in-law David had his middle name officially changed from Perry to Gerry on his birth certificate. It's not Jewish tradition to take the name of someone who's still alive, but it made me feel good. It was the best present imaginable. He framed a blow-up of the actual certificate, and I put it on my bedside table.

Cott had its annual meeting on June 17. The night before, Nancy made a beautiful party in our garden. She had a huge tent put up and invited all the Cott directors and their wives. We had a band, and everyone sang and danced. I sang "Splish Splash, I Was Taking a Bath." I sounded better than Bobby Darin.

What I will remember forever is my beautiful Nancy picking up a microphone and speaking to everyone from the heart. It floored me. It was better than sex. She is rising to the occasion. Then for the finale everyone circled around me as I sat on a chair, with my dog, Sophie, sitting on top of me. Everyone sang, "That's What Friends Are For." I was so overwhelmed that I couldn't even cry.

◆ ◆ ◆

The Cott annual meeting was a triumph. I entered the auditorium like a boxer before the big fight. My brother Sam gave me a white terry-cloth robe with "Cott" written on the back, as well as a pair of boxing gloves with my name on them.

I loved the idea of creating that kind of excitement and theatre. It's part of the "Go big or go home" philosophy. But I don't really see myself as a fighter. Sure, I'm a fighter when my back is against the wall. Then you don't want to deal with me. But I really think of myself as a lover. A fighter enters the ring alone. Most of my success has come from creating interdependencies with people. Only fools create adversarial relationships. The way to succeed is to get people on your team.

It was the most triumphant entrance I've ever made. I came into the room, punching the air, with the theme from the movie *Rocky* in the background. The crowd rose to its feet. I was so charged up by the time I reached the podium, swinging my arms around, that I accidentally hit my brother in the nose.

The first thing I did was have everyone hold hands and sing my favourite song, "That's What Friends Are For." I thanked my family, who were all in the front row. I reported a profit of $34 million on sales of over $1 billion. Then I talked about the future. About the bottling plants we were building in Tampa, Florida, and Wilson, North Carolina. And that we were going to reinstate the dividend we stopped paying out at the time of the restructuring. It's strange. The company is clearly back on track, ready for the next round. But I feel as though I've moved on.

The next day, I woke up early and waited to see what the newspapers had to say about the meeting. They were great, very positive. If ever anybody wasn't saying bad things about me, it was then. Why did they have to wait for me to get sick? Better late than never, I guess.

◆　◆　◆

I'm trying to come to terms with my spirituality. Just after my surgery, Barry Borden, our company doctor and my good friend, suggested I talk to Rabbi Dow Marmur of the Holy Blossom Temple. This is new territory for me. When I was growing up, my family was not particularly observant. We went to synagogue once a year for the High Holidays. I went through a phase around the time of my bar mitzvah when the idea of Gerry the Reform Rabbi started to appeal to me. I guess I was pleased I was able to do the whole service myself.

But a big part of it was the rebel in me, trying to shock my parents. When I was a teenager, once I broke the fast on Yom Kippur with Chinese food. Another year, I went out to a restaurant and ate steak and chips. Just so someone should catch me there. But despite those pranks, I take pride in belonging to the Jewish culture. Passover, Rosh Hashanah, and Hanukkah are all wonderful holidays to bring families together. I think the idea of sitting shiva for seven days is valuable to the family. It forces the family to figure out some of their problems.

I guess if I had to think about it, I'd say there's a supreme being out there who influences our lives. Certainly each move I've made in my life has been for a reason, even if those reasons weren't clear at the time. Sure, you'd have to ask, if there is a God, how would he allow something like this terrible thing to happen to me? But you also have to have confidence that the answer doesn't have to be found out now, that it will be found out later. I take comfort in that.

Rabbi Marmur is one of the smartest guys I've ever talked with. He said a lot of things that left a big impression. The first was "You know, I've seen more happy people in hospices than I've seen in board rooms." Then he said that no one can ever find peace with themselves or with others unless they were truly happy with themselves. There's no way you'll be happy until you can chase out these venomous parasitic things in your head.

That had a big effect on me. Because there's always been this guy in my head, yelling at me every day and every night in my sleep or in my office or my car or wherever else, judging me, saying, "This is wrong," "Don't do this," "You could have done it better," or "You could have done it this way." And it wasn't just business. It would be asking, "Why don't you spend more time with Clarke?" It was constantly second-guessing me, pointing out my self-destructive streak. That judge has been pretty hard on me for some time. I had to control everybody, but this guy in my head controlled me.

I realize now I'm trying to replace him with God. And I need help to do that. I know peace is coming from learning that you don't need to control everything to be happy. You don't need to manage everybody else's problems. I would invent things if I had nothing to do or worry about. I took over this job from my father, but I don't want it any more. I was the problem solver for

189

my brother Sam, problem solver for everybody who worked for me. I never gave myself time to solve my own problems. I've spent most of my life looking after others, including my children and my family. Maybe it's time for them to look after me. It's not something I'm going to be able to do easily. I have to release this judge in my head. Rabbi Marmur explained that until I was able to release it, I wouldn't be able to deal with any other problems.

Not long after I saw Rabbi Marmur, I received two books in the mail from Nelson Peltz, who had heard about my surgery when it was announced over the Bloomberg news service. Nelson is the chairman of Triarc, which bought Royal Crown after Victor Posner was forced out. It markets Snapple and Royal Crown Cola. He told me that these books did him a lot of good. So. I figured, getting up in the morning takes three minutes or whatever it is, and saying a few prayers and putting on a tallis, a prayer shawl, and a tefillin on my arm and head. Tefillin are long leather straps with a small square box on each. The boxes contain tiny parchments with the four passages from the Old Testament in Hebrew. I've been told that when I'm wearing tefillin God's radiance falls on me and wards off harm.

◆ ◆ ◆

About ten days before I got sick I had a dream about my father and all the people who came to his funeral. It made me wonder if I was as worthy a guy as he was, and if that many people would come to my funeral. I can't remember now whether the place was empty or whatever in the dream. But I came to the conclusion that the answer was no.

But when I got sick and the news was announced on Bloomberg and then in the papers, I received hundreds and hundreds of cards and baskets and flowers. From everywhere came fantastic beautiful letters from customers, from suppliers, from friends, from people I hadn't seen since high school. I even got a letter from the father of my first girlfriend, Rima. Heather Reisman called. Ron McKinley, who ran the Canada Deposit Insurance Corporation, has called me twice. Of all of the trust companies that failed in the 1980s in Canada, ours was the only one who paid back depositors 100 cents on the dollar. Bob Rae, the former premier of Ontario, wrote me a very kind note. I got a card from the executive vice-president of Kmart in the States. It made me realize how many things I've done, and how many people's lives I've been a part of. It made me realize that people do appreciate me.

At the end of June I got the most surprising letter of all. It was from Larry King. I've never met the guy. I rarely watch his show. But his letter said it was his pleasure to tell me that I had been nominated to receive the Theodor Herzl Award during a solidarity mission to Israel he was to lead in the third week of August. It's being organized by the Jerusalem Fund for the Aish HaTorah, which is their fundraising arm. I laughed when I read it. Do they know who they're honouring? The guy who was expelled from Hebrew school when I was twelve for making a paper plane out of a photo of Theodor Herzl and shooting it across the room. Then I read a line from Herzl on the invitation that surprised me: "If you will it, it is not a dream." That's exactly how I have lived my life.

191

I'm being honoured with an impressive group. There's also former secretary of state George Schultz, Minnesota Senator Rudy Boschwitz, Senator Orrin Hatch, and John Kluge, the chairman of Metromedia, and a bunch of high-profile business leaders. Fran Drescher, the star of *The Nanny* television show, is also receiving an award.

It's an amazing schedule. The award was to be presented by Prime Minister Benjamin Netanyahu, Jerusalem Mayor Ehud Olmert, and Larry King at Chagall Hall of the Knesset. They had a fantastic week-long program worked out. One day everyone was to be picked up by private helicopter for a tour of Petra, then on to King Hussein's palace in Amman for a private dinner with the king and his wife. They also planned to take us on a private tour of the Dead Sea Scrolls.

I'm not kidding myself about the award. If you showed this invitation to a gentile he'd probably be impressed and say, "Wow, you're going to meet the prime minister and the president and the king." Show it to a Jew and he'll say, "How much did you pay for it?" But I see it as an opportunity. It might be a chance to get a little bit of teaching that I wouldn't normally come across. It's also a chance to take my family to Israel. I went about ten years ago. Maybe Clarke could learn something from them too.

The days are flying. It's number twenty-three since my surgery. I just learned that Larry Grossman died. He was a lawyer and former provincial treasurer and Conservative party leader of Ontario. He was in his early fifties, and the only person I knew personally who had what I have. Hearing about his death was tough. I ask myself every day after my surgery, Am I so many days closer to here or closer to there? I think I'm closer to where I started. I still feel good. I haven't lost my appetite yet. I went out with my family the other night for deli.

I'm trying to get five days out of one. My schedule is packed. I'm up at six in the morning. Last night I sat up talking to my family until after midnight. I enjoy every second I spend with my grandsons. I took Jesse to see the movie *Batman*, which he loved. Then we went to Dairy Queen.

But I'm starting to feel the effects of the radiation. I get tired easily. My eyes close when I'm in the middle of a conversation. Even so, I went to a meeting for the operations group of Cott and spoke to the team. I have a lot of confidence that they will rise to the occasion.

One of my friends has an interesting theory. He understands the complexity of my personality—that I'm both the father and the kid, and that the kid has always been a big part of what made Gerry run. That's the side that never takes no for an answer. The part of me that's always walking on the ledge, close to the edge. For instance, I've never travelled with money. Either I'll go to a place where they know me and they'll send me a bill. Or there's somebody with me who can pay the bill. Whenever I would fly commercial it was a disaster. I'd forget my passport, my driver's licence. People would have to vouch for me. I'd lose gold Mont Blanc pens the way other people misplaced their Bics.

Five days after my surgery I scared Nancy by taking out my Ferrari and driving myself to Toronto Western Hospital to have my staples taken out. The Ferrari was another dream of mine, something I had to have. It goes two hundred and something miles an hour, or pretty fast, anyway. And now it's sitting in the garage.

193

I'm also thinking about the difficulty I have letting my friends take care of me. All I can think about is how to manage Cott from the grave, how to manage my family from the grave. I think, What kind of good guy is my wife going to get her hands on? I joke about her going to hook up with some cab driver. But it's not really a joke. It's fear on my part. I know it's wrong to think that way, but I can't seem to stop. I should give Nancy more credit than that.

That's part of the reason I hired Erik Dzenis to paint my portrait. He's painted Peter Bronfman's portrait, as well as a lot of the portraits in the lobby of the Princess Margaret Hospital. He came over to the house and took photographs for the preliminary sketches. It was my idea to wear a tuxedo. I've joked about this picture. I told everyone that I want it to hang in a prominent position with about two hundred pounds of explosives hard-wired to it. That way, if anyone tried to move it, the house would blow to smithereens.

Maybe that's why I am so calm about this. I've spent a lot of my life thinking about how people will remember me after my death. I never expected to have a long life. I would tell people that. I've always been concerned about how people would remember me. I visualized what life would be when I wasn't around any more, and in a strange way that has given me a greater peace.

I've been thinking about filming my own eulogy and having it played at my funeral. I'd just be sitting back in a big chair smoking a cigar, telling everybody how lucky I've been. How lucky I am.

◆ ◆ ◆

I wonder how long I'll be able to keep up this pace. I went to see *Jolson: The Musical.* The music was fantastic, all his hits like "Swanee," "Sonny Boy," and "Mammy." And what a life. Jolson left his Lithuanian rabbi father's house when he was eleven to join a circus. The thing about Jolson was his amazing ability to make himself likeable, whatever he did. He had great rapport with every audience. That fascinated me. It was the best show I've seen in years. Now I want to take my kids. They'll love it.

Yesterday Lawrence Bloomberg came over to the house with Larry Tanenbaum. They had a proposition. Lawrence is the head of First Marathon and a good friend. I've known him since Montreal. We went to Northmount High School together. In those days everyone called him Lawrie. Now that he's really successful, he insists everybody call him Lawrence. But he'll always be Lawrie to me. He's always been a really aggressive guy. He had very high standards and he's very tenacious. He's been involved in a lot of Cott's financings over the years and he's given me a lot of good advice. He and his wife, Fran, are great friends of ours. He's a guy I trust.

Larry Tanenbaum is a major player in the construction business and well known for his ownership investments in professional sports franchises, including a stake in the Toronto Maple Leafs. Larry and his wife, Judy, have been great friends of ours for a long time. He and Bloomberg had heard about my wanting to set up a foundation for brain tumors, and they wanted to make a pitch on behalf of Mount Sinai Hospital, where both are very active fundraisers. Their idea had something to do with naming rights to the hospital in exchange for a very large donation. Bloomberg and Tanenbaum are great guys and great friends of mine but their pitch really reflects how desperate and badly run the hospitals are. I'm learning that the medical system in Canada is just as screwed up as the business system. There are exceptions, of course. I've had nothing but great care at Toronto Western and Princess Margaret.

But what I've learned is that there's a whole power base in this world that I never realized existed, in the universities. It's as big as the government and even more political. I'm starting to find out that they play a very important role in how all these things are run. I'm sure they have good intentions. The professors and people who have seniority and tenure and all these people who are then out working as volunteers. All they're interested in is getting your money under their control so they can get a 4 per cent annuity off it, so it gives a researcher $40,000 a year. All that does is give the universities and hospitals more power.

I'm discovering that politics and bureaucracy are everywhere. Toronto has a first-class medical system, with great people, great research, but the different hospitals still can't put it together and share the same values. Everybody is fighting for turf. It's like "trauma is mine, heart is yours, amputation of the left leg is over here, the right leg is over there."

The system isn't run for efficiency. It sure isn't run for the benefit of patients. Instead, it's organized according to what's politically correct, what satisfies the status quo, for the guys who are running the show. All they want is a big endowment and more and more power in their hands. And all the bureaucracy and red tape makes it impossible to make a difference.

What really opened my eyes to it was when I went out and looked for someone to help me to write a mission statement for the foundation. We got one of the most senior people at one of the major hospitals. We just took for granted that he was helping us. Then a week later it was apparent he had a big conflict of interest when he came back with a recommendation that the foundation should be funded in a way that benefited his hospital.

So I went to Alan Hudson, the CEO of the Toronto Hospital. He's a smart guy. He invited me for lunch and I gave him my vision of this foundation. Then I told him that I'd like to meet someone who can give me some help to create a mission statement and focus the operation. He introduced me to Jim Stonehouse, a consultant who used to work for them, and he did some work for Barrick Gold. I gave him the material we've collected and he said that he'd go over it and come back to me with some ideas.

Anyway, yesterday after my radiation, I returned to my house for a meeting with Stonehouse. I couldn't believe the sight waiting for me. Sitting in my living room was Alan Hudson. With him was my family, Mark Bernstein, and, with a huge palm blocking his face, there's Fred Eaton. He's one of the Eaton brothers who own the Eaton's department stores, which are having such a hard time right now. Fred is also the president of Toronto Hospital and has a lot of clout in the political and medical communities.

I felt like I was being ambushed. They made a pitch for me to be giving them $7 million or $8 million for the Neuro Sciences at Toronto Hospital.

I'm sure if I told Mr. Eaton I'd give him $10 million, he'd phone the prime minister and make sure that I got the Order of Canada before I died. But that holds zero interest for me. The establishment here has very little to offer, in my opinion. There are exceptions, like Conrad Black, who I think is a very smart guy, even though I don't always understand what he's going on about. But at least he's interesting.

Last week I was invited for dinner with the prime minister

and the queen. I didn't go. It wasn't because of my illness. It's because that crowd has nothing to offer. They have different values. None of them ever made a dime on their own steam. They have no idea what it's like to go out and make a buck.

◆ ◆ ◆

There's something really wrong with the attitude toward success in Canada. I was reminded of it when I appeared on the television show *Canada AM* in the last week of June. The woman who interviewed me seemed nice enough, but she set up the interview in a negative way. "By any measure," she said, "Gerry Pencer has had a turbulent decade. In 1987 Financial Trustco crumbled under his watch. After he returned to Cott, he ran into a spot of trouble." Then she talked about how the stock price has declined. It amazes me that people still focus on the negative when the fact is that we took two tigers by the tail in Canada. That we outsell Coke and Pepsi in most supermarkets is incredible. The reality is that the stock price has risen in less than ten years from 16 cents to $14 now. That's a great success.

I explained to her that in Canada we tend to eat our own. Americans take great pride in their entrepreneurs and reward them. It amazes me that after building up a world-class business that takes Canadian technology and exports it all over the world, that creates $2 billion of market cap, and the Canadian press asks you, "Why is it now only a billion? You must be a big failure." What about the fact that you went from $10 million to $1 billion in the end? It's hard to understand. I told her the stock was up eight times from the time that I came to the company. All this is just a continuing evolution of the business. It's been a very successful business since the first day. I explained to her that I was focusing on being a manager, making tough decisions. I realized when I was talking to her that my whole life I've been restructuring. This tumor just gave me my latest opportunity to restructure.

◆ ◆ ◆

So here's a typical Gerry Pencer situation. Two days after I did the *Canada AM* interview, I went to Vegas to see the Tyson–Holyfield fight. The idea was to have some fun with my family and to relax. Twelve hours later I was hiding under a slot machine in the MGM Grand trying to avoid a human stampede.

It started well enough. We flew to Vegas on Friday morning. I took the kids. Clarke invited his new girlfriend, Christina, who lives in Ottawa. Mike Tyson chartered the Cott plane after he was released from jail in 1995. I wanted to have lunch in Denver, but my doctors said that the high altitude might pose a problem for the pressure in my head. So we spent Friday just relaxing in Las Vegas. We stayed at Caesar's Palace. We played blackjack together. I won $3,000. I gave each of my kids $500 to spend. My family hung out at the Forum Shops at Caesar's. The fountain outside the Versace boutique is nicer than the Trevi Fountain in Rome.

The fight was worth $30 million to Tyson, $35 million to Holyfield. I bet $1,000 on Holyfield. The thing with Tyson is that you never know what he's going to do next. The whole Kid Dynamite thing. He grew up with idolizing pimps and thieves. By the time he was ten he was mugging old ladies and shooting into crowds for kicks.

We got there at about four-thirty for the preliminary bout of women's boxing. The actual fight was eight o'clock. The ring is part of the MGM Grand hotel, but it's in an amphitheatre of its own and you have to go through the casino to get to it. Each ticket cost $5,000. I took Nancy, David, and Clarke. The girls stayed back in the hotel. Nancy was excited because she figured she was going to see all these movie stars. It was quite a scene. What struck me the most were the different camps. The Tyson fans were rap stars, pimps, and motorcycle gang members. The women were amazing. There must have been two tons of injected silicone in that auditorium. Some of them were fantastic-looking and even the ones who were ugly created a stir because of how outlandish they looked. The Holyfield people were more mainstream. Holyfield gives a large portion of the money he makes to a foundation to support inner-city kids. He's a really good man.

We sat in the eighth row, right behind Donald Trump and his entourage. Madonna was there. So were Rodney Dangerfield, Larry Flynt, Michael J. Fox, and Roseanne with her husband. Even Sylvester Stallone was there. The *Baywatch* guy David Hasselhoff was on our side. James Caan was right next to us. So was JFK Jr.

The actual fight didn't last very long. After Tyson bit Holyfield's ear, he turned toward Trump, grabbed his crotch, and made an obscene gesture in Trump's direction. I don't remember any reports of the fight writing about that. The minute that happened I could tell the place was heading out of control. I've been through scary moments, but this was the scariest. And now I was out of control because I was sick. I felt the need to defend my people and get them out of there as quickly as possible. But I couldn't move. Everything was jammed. I was walking with Anthony Munk, the son of Peter Munk, who runs Barrick Gold. Anthony works for Gerry Schwartz. We met him in the arena unexpectedly. He was there to meet two people who never showed up. It seemed we had to walk two hours to get from the auditorium to the casino. That's when we heard popping noises like guns going off.

That's when the stampede began. It was like watching the bulls run at Pamplona. My family was starting to run and I stopped them and put them underneath me. Clarke and Nancy and I were under a slot machine. David was right next to us, under the dice table. When the kids were young, we used to do what we called the Pencer family sandwich. Nancy and I would be the bread and the kids were various kinds of fillings. This was nothing like that. I was terrified. I also was starting to get claustrophobic, which made everything worse. I already have one bullet in my head, I kept saying to myself. Another one I don't need.

We didn't get back to the hotel room until four in the morning. The girls were all crying. They had heard that five people had been killed at the hotel. I spent all of the next day in bed. Twenty-four hours later I was still scared. I have never been so happy to go home in my life.

When I got back I met with the executive committee at Cott. I know I'm working too hard. I need to slow down. But I can't, even though the cure is making me sicker. The radiation treatments are getting to me. I'm also taking large doses of steroids. I'm getting tired and have less strength. My legs are getting weaker. Radiation is also giving me a metallic taste in my mouth that's really unpleasant.

We also had a party for our housekeeper, Cris Cruz, who became a Canadian citizen in the first week of July. Cris has been with us for years. She always has a kiss and a hug for me. We made a party for her at a Filipino restaurant. Nancy invited forty-five of Cris's friends. I caught wind of the fact that Cris had hired a stripper for me. I hate that sort of thing, so I decided to turn the tables. I arranged to hire a male stripper for her. He showed up in a Toronto policeman's hat and an outfit and told Cris there were problems with the citizenship papers. Then he handcuffed her to her chair. She loved it. Then he rolled out his routine, and when he took off his hat, he had this hair down to there. He ended up wearing the Canadian flag. If you need a good stripper, he was one. All my kids were there, singing along to the karaoke machine. It's the kind of social event I like best. I don't have to prove anything. I can be myself. If anything I'm driving for right now with my sickness it's that I want to be myself. I've always been myself but even more so now.

Later that night we drove up to the Cott-age, our name for our compound on Lake Joseph in Muskoka. We bought it in 1993 and my family has had some of its best times together there. Around the time it came up for sale, I was actually thinking of buying the Sherwood Inn, a great resort right next door. Don't even ask me why. It seems like a crazy idea now.

We love the Cott-age. It's our refuge. It's a beautiful place, done in the old Muskoka style with a huge main house over the boathouse, with two separate cottages and big decks on three levels. We treat it like a resort. There's staff and six boats—a canoe, two jet skis, a paddle boat. The house is run by Terry Ledger. She's fun-loving and I love talking with her. She takes great care of me. My favourite thing is a fantastic audiovisual system that includes a screen that descends from the ceiling above the fireplace. When you turn it on, speakers rise up out of the floor. Outside the speakers are disguised as rocks. My big idea was an overlook from the roof with a blue canopy over it. The neighbours complained that it blocked their view. It all ended up in court. We lost.

Not long after we bought it, my brother-in-law Steve and his wife, Andrea, and daughters, Ilana and Sara, showed up with an almost life-size wooden cut-out of a moose as a house-warming gift. We put it on a floating dock that we swim from. I decided to name the moose after my mother-in-law, Claire, so we had *Claire* painted on it. When my mother-in-law came up I gave her binoculars so she could see it. She knows I love her and I know she has a good sense of humour.

Since I've been sick I've had my best times with my family and our close friends up here. David's father, Henry, came for a visit. So has Fraser Latta and his wife, Heather. Fraser wants to see the company continue, but on the personal side, he'd like to spend more time with his family. He's only forty-three. Before I got sick, he cut his work back to three days a week. He wanted to leave last year but I wouldn't let him. After my surgery, he came back full-time to help me out. Fraser has always been incredibly loyal.

Nancy's brothers and their families were also up for a week-end. One of the best things about going to the Cott-age was stopping along Highway 11 at Webers, a place famous for its charcoal-broiled hamburgers. Now they taste bad because of my radiation.

This weekend *The Financial Post* wrote a big story about me. The head was "Defending Your Life." The story about me went over the same territory all stories about me go over, but it was generally pretty balanced. My son-in-law was angry that they can't let the past go. It didn't really bother me. I've seen so much worse. Of course I would have hoped it celebrated the success of my life, but they won't do that, so what can I do?

It's wonderful being with the kids, but I'm really exhausted and have constant queasiness. I have a new bond with pregnant women. I just found out I can get marijuana for the nausea. My speech is not great, but I'm sure that's because of the high dose of steroids I'm taking. My concentration is not good but it's okay. I don't enjoy watching television any more. I just can't concentrate. I also worry that the mask they put on me for radiation is getting tight. I worry about my head swelling.

The radiation has knocked out my saliva glands and that now makes it more difficult to talk. We had a beautiful barbecue for dinner but all I craved was potato chips and a hot dog. The salt is the only thing that cuts through. My stomach was acting up, so I got Barry Borden, Cott's doctor, to drive over from his cottage, which is twenty miles away and give me a double shot of Gravol. The next day I still felt sick and stayed in bed all day. Is this what I have to look forward to? Someone ordered pizza, but I didn't want any. But I believe I'm getting better. I'm starting to write better, even though my writing is horrific. I can't spell two words straight. I can't write down someone's phone number.

Yesterday I received a call from a cousin by marriage who was just diagnosed with the same type of cancer I have. He's only fifty-one. He's having his surgery next week. So of course I had to get involved and call my surgeon, Mark Bernstein. I make a point of talking to him a lot. I'm in this guy's face, I know. But you have to look at it this way. He loses I don't know how many patients a year. I'm going to make him realize there's a person that's bigger than the tumor.

◆ ◆ ◆

I can't stop worrying about Cott. I want to leave a legacy that's permanent and not just a pile of paper. Cott is a real company. It's tangible. There's a big difference between shuffling paper and making things. You tend to look at paper shuffling in the shorter term. But a manufacturing company should have legs for the longer term. Our people are very capable. But I've been the daddy for a long time. And they've worked well with the nurturing I've given them and my management style. When I see a lot of people who work for me, they give me a kiss. That's unusual in this day and age. That's the kind of place it is. But a business cannot survive for long being run by a committee. It's time for this company to march on. One reason I don't want to go into the office is that these guys have to learn to run a business on their own. I need to get my mind around this. But it's really hard. I can't resist telling people how they should be running the business and restructuring things.

I haven't phoned many people since I've been sick but I have started. I phoned John Thompson at Loblaws. He was happy to hear from me. I'm thinking of going to go and see Safeway probably next week because we have an important contract negotiation with them. I need to help.

True and Elizabeth Knowles came to see me after I underwent some horrendous tests at the hospital. True is willing to come to Cott full-time. He'd bring a lot to the company, but he's a lot different in his approach than I am. He's tough and methodical. He's the general. It's going to be painful to people. There's a lot of confusion right now.

Nancy gave me a new pen inscribed "The Shadow of Your

205

Smile Forever." That was the song we first danced to at our wedding reception. When she gave it to me, it made me cry.

◆ ◆ ◆

Danny Silver has put together extensive files on everything about brain cancer. Some of it seems legitimate, but you've got to be careful because there are so many quacks out there selling hope. It's no different than bust-enlarging cream. It's a matter of mind over matter. Most alternative medicines don't work, but there is something for everyone, including the little cream.

One of the people from my security company gave me a book called *Sharks Don't Get Cancer*. The thinking is that shark cartilage is supposed to suppress the tumor's blood vessels. I took the stuff for a while, then I stopped. I don't think it does any good. I've also been drinking boatloads of Essiac tea, which tastes awful but is supposed to cure all kinds of cancers by boosting the immune system.

Everyone wants to tell me about the latest theory. My son-in-law told me about this idea that if you can keep your body in a high alkaline state and reduce the acid, cancer can't grow. There's also acupuncture and alternative Chinese medicine. I've met an interesting doctor, Dr. Chow, through Mark Bernstein, who trained him as a surgeon. But he opted out. Now he's got a drug company that specializes in Eastern drugs. I went to see him last Tuesday. He has anti-oxidant drugs that are supposed to improve the immune system.

One of the most promising things emerged from a meeting David set up with Rebecca Keeler at Dimethaid Research. I went with him, Nancy, and a fellow with Mark Bernstein's group. The company went public on the TSE and raised

$30 million this year. They've come up with SRT 101, an interesting drug that boosts the immune system. It's given to you intravenously every day for five hours for five days and then hopefully it sends a different message to confuse the tumor, which prevents its growth.

The idea is that I'd take chemotherapy once a month. Then once a week I'd take SRT 101. I'd have to take it for the rest of my life. It's usually been used to treat AIDS. The strength of your immune system determines how much chemo you can take. It's had good results on rats but hasn't been approved by the FDA or the Canadian government. It's still in its clinical phases. I've applied to the government to use it on compassionate grounds. My doctors are willing to let me have it as soon as I'm off radiation. I expect to get approval in the next few weeks. It's something I have to get.

◆ ◆ ◆

This is a non-stop situation and it hasn't ended. It's always churning, twenty-four hours a day. Here I want to help this cousin now who has the same illness. His surgery turned out well, but he needs help getting through it.

The rabbi tells me I have to be happy with myself, and he's right. I have to chase out the demon. And I tried for a few days, but then it seems that I'm looking for more punishment. I like the word *punishment*. It means that some illicit danger has gone before it. It's like setting up the foundation. Who knows what kind of fight I'm going to cause in the Toronto community over the medical system? I want to be an enabler here to these people in non-major centres to get them to where they need to be to maximize their opportunity to survive.

A big part of this is that I want to share, and I want to help people. But at the back of my mind I also know I want to help myself. I want to live. It's one thing to say that you're not afraid to die, and I don't think I am. Well, maybe a little bit, because no one really knows what you face when you die or where you're going, if anywhere. But even with as much as I've already accomplished, I want to live for as long as I can, with the quality that you need to go with it. It's one thing to have the willingness to share, but before that you need the ability to write a cheque for what you want to share, which kind of helps.

And while this is 80 per cent philanthropic, there's still the old Gerry here with the other 20 per cent. The minute you say you're going to donate, you become the centre of the universe. I'll tell them what I'm going to put up, at least 10 per cent of my equity, they'll add it up and they'll figure that I'm going to put in at least $10 million to start with. Right away, all these guys are looking at me for how much money they can get out of me. And all of a sudden, I don't need an appointment, I don't wait for anyone. I've been able to get appointments on demand. Normally you would get an MRI every three or four months. I've already had three. I have access to experimental drugs, even though I'm not supposed to talk about it. There's definitely a little bit of difference in the standard.

But even though I'm getting preferred treatment, I have to say I've never seen such wonderful care as in the Princess Margaret and Toronto Hospitals. It's magnificent. The people are unbelievably compassionate. I don't think there's any better medical care anywhere in the world. We're very lucky. But do we appreciate it? No. People just bitch about the medical service. I know I'm getting under their skin. We sent the staff in the radiation unit of Princess Margaret Cott T-shirts, balloons, baskets of candy. Stacey organized a catered barbecue for them with salads, hot dogs, and a sundae bar. That's my style. Always needing to take care of everyone.

◆ ◆ ◆

My makeup is such that I'm going to get through this, but the reality of jumping over some of the stuff that I'm facing is hard, really hard. What I have to face frightens me. I have a new difficulty finding words. I figure it's a 10 per cent speech impediment. And since the surgery, I've had short-term memory loss; sometimes I can't remember what I had for breakfast. My arm shakes and I can't use my right hand. A lot of things worry me, based on what I've learned about my illness. Blindness for one. There's always the risk of paralysis as well. The thing that scares me the most is seizures. I'm terrified of losing control. I'll be starting chemotherapy after my next session of radiation. A lot of people lose a lot of their faculties as they go through it. The lucky ones come out of it at the other side. There's still lots of hope, but sometimes it's difficult to feel it. Today they found some errant cancer cells. It wasn't a surprise. That's why I'm taking radiation and all this stuff to kill it. But it's just one more thing, having to think about these little cells crossing over the line and then wanting to grow so quickly. It's a race here now between me and my supporters and the cancer.

The next phase of my treatment is something called stereo-tactical radiation, which allows precisely focused, high-dose beams to be delivered to the tumor site. It's another way to maximize the period that this goes into a remission. The sessions last about forty minutes each for five days. It's a relatively new treatment. Most people don't even know about it. They don't give it to everybody, but I'm a pretty demanding guy. They're selective. They still don't know how good it is. Because it's so focused, they have to fit you with a custom-made head frame that looks like a helmet. First, they do a CAT scan and MRI. The fitting process was torture for me. They put a bit plate in the back of your mouth that attaches to the bed to keep you still. You can't talk, you can't move, you can hardly breathe. I was totally claustrophobic as they rolled me into the CAT-scan machine. You can't ask for help. It took about three hours altogether to do the fitting. Then they tried to take blood in both arms and both failed because they couldn't find a good vein. What a mess. But I'm sure I'll get over it. I guess my challenges have to be made tougher and tougher because I'm so good at getting past them.

I want to get the foundation off the ground as soon as possible. Anyone else would be saying, "Can we get the doctors? Can we get the lawyers? What are the tax implications? Blah, blah, blah." You've got to forget all that. I want the foundation to break new ground, to help people directly. I want to get everyone involved—hospitals, universities. If my life in business has taught me anything, it's that when people are interdependent they'll work very hard toward a solution. I want to shake things up. I want to start a war.

Now I'm working with Alan Bernstein, the smartest scientist in Toronto, at the Lunenfeld Research Institute at the Mount Sinai Hospital. Even my own surgeon was reluctant to introduce me to a guy who works for him but who happens to be stationed at the Mount Sinai Hospital. Bernstein is not a bullshitter. He thinks that gene therapy is going to create a cure for cancer over the next five years. I wouldn't be surprised if he receives the Nobel Prize.

I'm trying to meet as many people as possible in the area. Sandy Aird introduced me to Diane Lister, the president and CEO of the Sick Children's Hospital foundation. She's a very smart, really impressive woman. She was very helpful. Holly and Nancy were with me. I can tell that they are really getting into this thing. They will be great assets.

I've talked to Michael Levine, and Hugh Segal, who's sort of a guru to the Tories. He used to be chief of staff for Prime Minister Mulroney. He grew up in my neighbourhood in Montreal, and he's a good guy. He's a director of Vincor, the wine operation Schwartz and I control. He knows everybody. We had a meeting the other day and I told him about my concern about people being skeptical about my involvement in this. I know there will be a bunch of dodos in the press who will take potshots, saying that I'm just being opportunistic. I'm worried my name will make people more doubtful and less helpful. I don't want them to think it's for my own self-aggrandizement, because it's not. Segal's response to my worries was classic. He said, "Reporters are people who come down from the hills with machine guns to shoot the wounded." I like that.

If I had my way, I'd leave my name out of it entirely. I don't want it to be formal. I want this to be approachable, fun. I was thinking I'd just call it BRAINS, like an acronym. It will become well known all over the medical establishment. Or I could call it Gerry's Brains. The only thing wrong with that is it sounds like something Jerry Lewis is involved in. I don't want to be side-swiped by cynics. I remember the storm of criticism when they named the faculty of management at the University of Toronto after Joe Rotman, who gave them a pile of money. I don't want anything for myself, but I still have to position this so that they can't look at it as my latest scheme.

I have learned that the federal government is willing to support private enterprise. It's a matching program. As long as the foundation is national in scope, they'll put up 40 per cent if the applicants put up the other 60. The hospital might put in as much as 20 per cent. So I imagine this thing could be worth $50 million. And the other 60 can come from philanthropic donors, from private companies, from provincial governments, from agencies like the National Cancer Institute of Canada. We could go to the Canada Foundation for Innovation and say we need money to buy a DNA sequencer that's $200,000. We also need to renovate some lab space, and we would like some money to recruit young scientists.

There are very few knowledge centres committed to dealing with this disease, probably because there is so little of it relative to other kinds of cancer. So the less research there is, the tougher it is to deal with it. I'm sure that's why there are so many misdiagnosed cases, because doctors are not properly trained to deal with it. If you want to give somebody the best shot at surviving a disease like this, you need to go to someone who specializes in it. Not only that, but the technology doesn't exist in very many places to support longer life. I want to help them with information, funding, better clinical care, and more support for families. We want a philosophy of a continuum of research and care, and if people don't want to be part of this larger objective, we're not interested. We want patient care to be the top priority. We want to provide continuity from the time people have the operation. As I see it, a lot of people fall off the radar screen after surgery. There's no follow-up. It's like doctors are afraid of the patients, they're afraid of failure. We figure that if we can improve patient follow-up we could improve the quality of their lives three times.

I also want to offer hope. One of the books I received was Bernie Siegel's *Love, Medicine and Miracles*. He's a critic of the medical establishment. He says that doctors should never say to you that there's no hope. They have to give you some hope, they have to try, there must be something different. You can't give up. I'm sure if 25 per cent of these people were just in a better frame of mind, there would be much better results. Nelson Peltz wants to introduce me to Bernie Siegel. Siegel's famous for saying things like "good health is the ability to do without it" or "my definition of a good patient is a bad patient," which really makes sense to me. I'm all for meeting him because he might give me a blurb for my book. Sometimes it really helps to be well connected. Nelson's also going to ask Mike Milken to call me. Mike started to talk about his foundation and the process he went through, not only the logistics of it but also just the emotional part of it. He started the foundation after his prostate cancer.

It's important to me that our facility is a place that's friendly to patients. I don't want it to look like a hospital. I only want to hire people who really care about people. The system doesn't focus on the living portion. I'm going to have social workers talking to families, figuring out how these people can fit into their new lives. I don't have to work, and I can afford anyone I need to help me. But most people still have to worry about making a living. How are they going to support themselves? That will be a very big part in helping these people. Otherwise they just have to pack it in.

One thing that became apparent is how separate all the various treatments are. I had my radiation therapy and then my stereotactical therapy, but there wasn't any integration. I want to have medicine, social work, nursing, clinical trials, medical imaging, and psychiatry under one roof. I figure that if it's integrated the results will be much better.

These guys are running a real business that they weren't before. I want to support other ventures coming to Toronto to create a network. What's the point of having a Centre of Excellence if no one else comes? I'm saying let patients at the Cleveland clinic come. In that way, we're going to use our infrastructure better. They have floors that are empty, all sorts of unused capacity, if you want to use the example of a bottling plant.

I want to appoint a scientific panel that will decide where the money will be spent. I don't want to fund one particular organization. So if somebody has some great idea in genetics, we might give him $1 million or $500,000 or whatever he needs to get these projects going.

I'm going to have only the best people on my board. That will give us credibility. Holly and Nancy have become involved as well. I want Holly to take an active role running it. She has been travelling to conferences and meeting people. Next week we have people coming in from a brain tumor foundation in the U.S. to meet with us and share information. The other thing I want to do is to sponsor a symposium once a year. It would be a think-tank of the brightest people in this field who could share information. Right now, there isn't a lot of money to get these people together. But I don't want my think-tank only to be made up of scientists. I also want X-ray and oncology people, surgeons. I want to integrate all the different areas. That's the only way you can succeed.

Mount Sinai can't get along with the other three hospitals because their identity is worth everything to them and they know that if they merge, or whatever, they're going to lose their brand-name. In a way I don't want them to merge, because the hospital is so important for the Jewish community, even though 80 per cent of the people treated there are not Jewish. But I want Sick Kids, Mount Sinai, and Toronto Western as part of it. There will be a clinical component, and a research component. We want to support everything from basic research to more complex research such as gene therapy as well as patient care and clinical aspects. There are very few places that can honestly say they are the very best in all those areas.

Obviously we need a home base. Once we figure out where it will be, I'd like to have my offices there. I'm going to need an executive director and I'm going to need probably one or two clerical people to help process all these requests. Where we finally set up is a bit of a pressure point with me because obviously I feel a commitment to the various hospitals that have helped me. But the other reality is that all the hospitals are getting closer together out of necessity because of cuts in government spending. So in the long run it may not matter. I don't know what noises the medical establishment are going to make about this approach in the short term, but I'm not worried about that. In my experience, people eventually get on with whatever they're doing. And I think if people feel that they've been fairly dealt with, then they don't complain. Anyway, it's my money.

I can't stop. It's as if I'm not happy unless I'm dreaming up another new idea. I even came up with a concept to raise money that will get Cott's customers involved in it. It's called Brain Cents and the idea is for retailers to donate a few pennies from each case of Cott beverages they sell and donate the proceeds to the foundation. It would also be great publicity for Cott.

If we decide ever to sell the company, which is not my plan, I will have a couple of hundred million more cash, so I'll take part of my cash flow from that to fund the thing. I would get them to make an agreement that they're going to continue for at least five years to fund it.

◆ ◆ ◆

I'm still wrestling with what I should do about Cott. Do I sell it? Do I keep it? Some people from Morgan Stanley have come up from New York with the best people from Deloitte Touche to meet with us to discuss all the alternatives. Lawrence Bloomberg is going to help me too. He just called me from his vacation in Capri.

I have really mixed feelings about whether to sell the family's stake. I've been the visionary there. Why should I leave it for someone to screw up? My family will have enough money. Even though my dad founded the company, I see the company as a first-generation corporation, not a second-generation company. It's a completely different company from what it was when I came. I know now that I was the only one who could have made that kind of difference. I don't think it matters whether a business is first or second generation. I think what you need to ask yourself is, Has this business been reinvented over the last generation?

I'm going to try my best to figure out a way of keeping the company in the family. I believe that children should not run businesses unless they are more capable than any other candidate. Most families are great at turning big fortunes into smaller ones. A business needs a leader who has vision and who has the drive to work hard and at the same time to inspire people to feel about the company as if it was their own. I guess it's every father's dream to have a child who's as interested as they are, but I'm not sure that's the case in this situation. My daughter Holly is driven, and she has a lot of my entrepreneurial instincts, but she's winding down her work at Cott to work at the foundation. Maybe that's controlling on my part, but that's what she seems to need to do. Clarke is only twenty-four. He still has visions of being in the entertainment business.

My son-in-law, David, could run Cott, but he's doing a great job at the private-label bleach company KIK, which is doing about $100 million in business a year. I believe it has the potential to do better than Cott, because there's only one competitor in the sector instead of two. I believe we're going to see a consolidation in the bleach business, which will mean there will only be KIK and Clorox. Right now we've got Clorox on the run. David has a lot of ability and the company needs to be entrepreneur-driven. David is too much like me. He's got to find his own way. I feel Cott is in good hands now. True is running the executive committee. Humberto is a very smart guy. Ted Zittel is going to be our next chief creative officer. He's been with Don Watt for twenty-some years. Mark Benadiba is running the operations of the business and he's a good guy, a really good guy. He's a street fighter like me.

To maximize value, I might need to break up the company. One option would be to spin off our American business and take it public. About 58 per cent of our business is based in the U.S. Then the Canadian parent would own 60 per cent. On its own it's worth a billion; it's more than the sum of the parts. And then I would let the shareholders in Canada take either cash or stock in exchange. What that would mean is that, instead of my family owning 30 per cent of the stock, we go up to 40 or 50 per cent in Canada, but we'd have less of a piece of the other. But you're putting yourself in a position that people can't bump you out.

The people I'm consulting think it's more important to keep a business like this intact. It is a truly great Canadian business. But I have to admit I'm less interested in Cott than I used to be because it's not the same business it was a few years ago. We're still a good marketer, but now our focus is on being a producer, manufacturer, and distributor. And we're doing a great job at that. But it doesn't turn me on as much as my earlier vision for the company. But as much as I say that and think that, deep down I don't want to sell Cott. And the reason is that in the back of my mind I want to go back there, as much as I'm saying I don't want to go back there. My ultimate victory would be to walk back into that place and take it over again. Then I'd sell it. Then I would have the choice.

I wonder what Cott is going to do without me. I'm very much a proponent of giving added value to our customer, and there aren't a lot of guys like that out there who are as committed as I am to doing that. I hear all the time that our customers miss me. The president of a major grocery chain, one of our biggest accounts, said to Mark Benadiba, "I hope you're half the man Gerry is." Just the other day I received a letter from Bob Anderson, who runs Wal-Mart's private brands division. He had a meeting with True Knowles and Mark Benadiba. And he said, "As good as the meeting was, Gerry's exciting vision wasn't there."

◆ ◆ ◆

I don't want to die as an enemy of my brother Sam. I'm busy worrying about him and his family but I must like it or I wouldn't

218

do it. I've been taking care of him for twenty years. I don't want to take care of him any more. I'm trying to work things through with my brother Bill. I see his kids, Max, Richard, and Gary, but now I'm seeing more of him too, much more. I've seen him probably once a week or once every two weeks since I've been sick. I feel more comfortable with him. We used to go months without talking, even though my wife is good friends with my sister-in-law, Ida. Of all things, she's a sex therapist with a practice at the Jewish General Hospital in Montreal. Bill sat with my management team the other day. I think he was shocked with how good things are at Cott. Later we had dinner together. We spent two hours, which is more than he has spent with me in fifty years. Mending things with Bill has been one of the biggest blessings of my illness. This judge that I have always had in my head isn't as loud as it was.

My other focus is helping my family through my illness. It's been devastating for them. Nancy and my kids can't accept the fact that I'm not going to be better. They love me and I know that. But them not accepting makes it more difficult for me, not easier. They want to be upbeat, so every scrap of news they hear that's good, they make a fuss about. I don't know what they talk about when I'm not around. Maybe they're more realistic. I hope so. I've always been honest with my kids. I cry in front of them. We don't have any secrets. There are no two conversations that go on at the dinner table. I'll say anything in front of them, including some off-colour or off-the-wall things. If I tell them I'm going to smoke a joint or something like that to deal with my nausea, I'd probably invite them to have one with me. That's just the way I am. I don't think I did as good a job of parenting my kids as my parents did with me. I travelled a lot. I wasn't there. Nancy handled so much. Stacey and David are much better parents to their two boys. They have the same attitude that my parents had.

Some of my personal conflicts are very difficult for me right now. I wish I could let go, but I still have decisions about Cott, about what to do with Destination Products International. Dave Nichol, who was running it, has left the company. The division did about $50 million a year but we were losing about $10 million a year. Destination had more than a hundred products under development but not enough focus. Part of the problem was that at Loblaw Nichol owned the shelf. At Cott it was a constant battle to push some of his products onto retailers. Dave has very high-brow tastes, and that didn't always wash in the States. The world didn't need another pomegranate rib sauce. It was a $25-million experience, but Cott is still standing. I'm proud of that.

I can't stop worrying about how Dave will land after all this. I loved that guy.

Taking a trip with my family was another dream I had after I got sick. We've had some fantastic family holidays. I want this one to be the most memorable. My plan is to lease a yacht and visit some of the most beautiful places around the French and Italian Rivieras at the end of July for a couple of weeks. Then after the cruise, we'll go to Israel for the award from Aish Hatorah in the middle of August. It's amazing how things work out. I'll be finished my radiation therapy by then.

I have wonderful memories of Italy. Nancy and I first went to Italy in September 1989, after I started at Cott. We had been through the mill together, and things were finally starting to look up. We flew to Rome and drove down the coast, visiting romantic places—Capri, Positano. In Capri we went to a beautiful restaurant called Da Paulino in the middle of a lemon grove. I had fresh fettucine with fried zucchini blossoms. It was one of the best meals I ever had. I hope so much to enjoy that again. Nancy handled all the arrangements. She leased a 168-foot cruise ship called the *Intrepid II*. It's top of its class, with a staff of eighteen, and a gym. You could buy a nice house in Toronto for what it costs for two weeks. Nancy even booked a woman to give massages and manicures. She used to work for Adnan Khashoggi, so I guess she's seen it all.

Stacey has even talked my oncologist, Warren Mason, into coming along. That will make me a lot more comfortable. She went to him and said, "You've got to help my dad. And you'll have the greatest time of your life." She's a chip off the old block. This guy is going to have to keep me alive one way or another. And he's going to have a wonderful time. I enjoy seeing everybody have a nice time. I even invited my mother-in-law to join us in Israel. Warren's motivated to try really hard to keep me alive. The last thing these guys want to do is to get personally involved with their patients. The other day my surgeon, Mark Bernstein, told me that he's got a practice to look after, and I shouldn't call him twenty times a day. But I'm unrelenting.

I'm getting more symptoms. I'm more nauseated and have a little paranoia. I'm also flagging a lot, but then I consider the schedule I'm keeping. It would knock anyone out. A lot of it is the radiation. It's very unusual to take any more than an ordinary dose of chemo. I'm taking already three drugs. I'm finishing up stereotactical radiation. Then I begin taking the immune booster, the wonder drug I've received special dispensation to take. It's administered through an IV, so I get a nurse and I'll take it from midnight until four in the morning continuously.

Yesterday, just a few days before we're scheduled to leave, I had a seizure, one of the things I was afraid of. The medical term is an episode, but that sounds too civilized for what really happens. It starts before you understand what's going on. It's like being in prison. You are inside something that doesn't ever seem to end. You have no control whatsoever. I had one seizure. And then another. And then another. And another. Losing control like that terrified me. It turned my world upside down.

We called an ambulance and went to the hospital. Warren put me on another drug. But he says that's no assurance that I won't get other seizures. It made me realize how vulnerable I am. Little things like seeing my grandchildren become really important. I want to put thoughts aside for my own family, to make something special for them.

◆　◆　◆

It's a week later and we're on the boat. The *Intrepid II* is something else—the most fantastic boat I've ever seen, and I've seen some beauts. The guest book in the main public area is amazing: Jackie Collins, Sidney Poitier and his wife, Barbara and Marvin Davis, Michael Jackson's wife and baby, Barbara Walters. The captain, Gus Rankin, was also the captain of the *Lady Gislaine*, the yacht belonging to the Australian publishing baron's Robert Maxwell the night Maxwell took his final fall into the Atlantic. Gus is a great guy, and the world's greatest captain, but he's discreet. I figure he knows a lot more than he says he does.

Fraser, Mark, and Humberto and their wives are with us for

the first week, and the rest of my family will join me for the second. Clarke and his girlfriend, Christina, are with Nancy and me for the whole time. So is Warren, my doctor, and his friend Daniel from New York, who's a great guy. The first week was marred only by the fact that Humberto's wife broke a rib while she was fooling around in a rubber tube in the Mediterranean. We were lucky Warren was with us. We had to rush to a nearby hospital.

I'm not able to walk by myself now—my legs are weak because I can't eat. It's a vicious cycle. I even fell a few times, trying to go to the bathroom. I also feel my speech going. It's getting harder and harder to find words, even though I know what I want to say. The right words just don't come. Or they come out wrong. I'll say *sergeant* when I mean *surgeon*. The most difficult thing is that everyone wants a piece of the old Gerry, and I can't give them that. It makes me feel guilty. We talked about the company. I feel sad that there isn't someone with my creative spark to carry it on. Everything is undecided. I was sad to see them go. It felt like an ending.

Having my family arrive for week two was more emotional than I thought it would be. It was a beautiful day. The sky was blue like heaven. I cried with joy when they we met them in the port in Monte Carlo. Holly brought her friend, Lisa Berkowitz, who works at Cott. They were so excited to be there. They all cried, too. It's difficult for them to see me this way, so vulnerable. It's especially hard for Jesse, my grandson. I'm his "papa." That's what he calls me. He doesn't understand the changes in me but he loves me just as much.

The food on the boat is fantastic. You can get anything you want any hour you want, but I have no appetite. I tried to come out and have lunch on the deck but nothing appealed to me. I spend most of my days in my bedroom watching movies. Usually David and Jesse join me. There's a library of about three hundred videos on the boat. Westerns have always been my favourite. Maybe because I always related to the idea of the outlaw, forging new frontiers. When I was a kid, my dad and I would watch westerns together. I used to play the theme from *The Lone Ranger* on my gramophone over and over.

We docked in Capri. I wanted the kids to experience the beauty and romance of the island as Nancy and I have for so many years. Unfortunately I was too weak to get off the boat. But I absolutely insisted that Nancy go with the kids and show them around. I wanted them to go shopping and I gave them my credit card and said not to come back without lots of shopping bags. I also wanted Nancy to pick out something special for our nieces. She came back with gold bells they could wear around their necks that hopefully will bring them good luck and make them remember me always.

Holly and I have also been having good talks about the future of the business. I'm thinking we should do a two-litre jug of filtered water for Wal-Mart. It would fly off the shelves. I worry we've fallen behind in terms of innovation. We broke ground in private label but we missed the second wave, which is the creation of new products and categories. Without innovation, we're dead. Coke and Pepsi can always lower their prices. If you don't continuously reinvent yourself in any business, you won't have a business. I built Cott up bottle cap by bottle cap. Not many people build that way. I had an appetite to learn. I'll try anything. I ended up with a real bull, and I knew how to capitalize on it. I scared the shit out of everyone. There was no big plan. This was just Gerry.

The risk is just becoming a manufacturer. That's not the

business that I built. Now the time has passed me. I can never get the same leverage out of my capabilities. I have to reinvent myself again. If I don't, I'm going to die. If I don't get off my ass, I might as well say goodbye. If I don't, I won't live much longer. If I do, the chances are greater.

My family is remarkable. We laugh a lot, even through this. They went off to have dinner at La Chaumière, this great restaurant between Nice and Cannes. It's one of my favourites. The beef there is fantastic. Nancy didn't want to go without me. But I wanted her to go and for everyone to enjoy themselves. Giving other people happiness is important to me. It'll be time to pack it in when I can't any more. I know I have given my family joy. But I worry about how long I'll be able to do that. For the first time in my life I don't look forward to what's happening. I'm afraid of it.

They came back with a video of the evening. Everyone had a fantastic time. Stacey and Holly were in my room until five o'clock, very upset. This is so difficult for them. They need me still to be the father, and I can't be right now. I know the medication is affecting my moods. I think about what I'm going to do when I return to Toronto. That scares me. I don't feel I can talk to my family about it. I don't know where I fit in any more. Mark McKay, the ship's steward, was with us too. He's South African, and a great guy. He got Warren out of bed to come and talk with everyone.

The mood swings with these drugs are giving me whiplash. Just when I feel down, there's some wonder that helps me see beyond this illness. Today Nancy and I went on a boat tour of the blue grottos of Bonifacio, Corsica. Getting me anywhere is a production, but it was worth it. The water is turquoise. Just beautiful. Tonight David and I watched *Honeymoon in Vegas*, which is just so-so. I even had soup for dinner, which is more than I've eaten in weeks.

A few days before we were scheduled to go to Israel, I got a letter from Larry King that my office faxed to me. In it, he said his doctor won't allow him to travel because of a recent heart attack. He wants to be healthy to marry his fiancée. This is something like marriage number eight for him. So he won't be in Israel. That was one of my incentives for going. I feel as if I've been misled. He ended the letter by saying how much he regretted not being able to attend. He actually said, "I wish I were in your shoes." I doubt that. Now, though, I'm beginning to wonder about whether *I* can make it to Israel. Larry King not being a part of it is only one of the reasons. I am afraid of how I'm going to get around. How can I spend a week in Israel holed up at the King David Hotel waiting for the awards ceremony?

Last night, we went to one of the best restaurants in the world—Gallura in Olbia, on the island of Sardinia. Dave Nichol introduced Nancy and me to it on one of our trips. It's a truly great culinary experience. It took an hour by cab to get there. They had prepared a table for us upstairs, not knowing it is difficult for me to navigate steps. Captain Gus and one of the engine room guys came with us. I sat on a chair and they helped carry me up. The restaurant is family-style, with red-and-white tablecloths. We started with octopus salad, then oysters and clams with grappa, fried calamari, shrimp, linguine con vongole with a caviar. I shut my eyes to taste it. Then there was lobster, and a round of pecorino romano cheese. I ended the meal with a cigar. Rita Denza, the owner and cook, gave us a bottle of grappa and a round of pecorino. I asked her to remember me, for when I came back.

◆ ◆ ◆

God works in mysterious ways. Just when I'm trying to figure out whether I can go for this big award in Israel, who do I get an audience with but Pope John Paul II. Different team, maybe, but I need all the spiritual good will I can get these days. Bill Avery, the chairman of Crown Cork and Seal in Philadelphia, set it up. Bill has been a friend for years. His company is the largest packaging company in the world and supplies all Cott's cans. We're their second-largest customer. Bill's a real high-quality guy. He came to visit me at my house in late June, about a month after my diagnosis. That's when he first brought up the idea of me having an audience with the Pope. He gives a lot of money to the Catholic Church. Bill says the Pope gives off a glow that fills you with awe.

We received a letter outlining the ground rules. It said I could take four guests. I asked that David be included. I think of him as my son. We were told the men should wear dark business suits and the women must wear dark colours and cover their heads and arms. If you address him, you have to call him either "Your Holiness" or "Holy Father." He was at Castel Gandolfo, the Pope's official summer residence, southeast of Rome. We had to change course to arrive at a port outside of Rome first thing in the morning. It was a difficult passage. It took seven hours and everyone came down with a bit of seasickness. We got up at four-thirty for an hour-and-a-half drive. I ended up taking seven people: Nancy, Holly, Clarke, Stacey, David, Warren, and Clarke's girlfriend, Christina. The town square was filled with Swiss Guards. We met Richard Krzyanowski, who works for Crown Cork and Seal, and had breakfast.

The doors opened at seven, so we had to wait in an open

corridor lined with windows and shutters. It was beautiful, filled with frescoes and Murano glass chandeliers and statuary. The corridor let out onto a balcony with a view of lakes and the hills of Rome. We waited and then moved to the chapel. There were four nuns and eight priests wearing white with red crosses. The floors were marble inlaid. The altar was marble, too, topped with gold candlesticks. Above it there was a picture of Mary and Jesus, wearing gold crowns. The Pope entered from a huge door on the right of the chapel. He's not in such great shape himself. He had a hard time opening the door. Then a couple of priests dressed him in a white robe with a red sash. He didn't look at us. His voice was low and hoarse. He had to sit down for part of the service. There were a couple of other people in there with us. One man was in a wheelchair. I heard a rooster in the background.

It was an experience unlike any other I've ever had. I was holding Nancy's hand. The tears streamed down my face. I saw a kaleidoscope of colours, brilliant colours swirling around. I felt the spirit of the place. When the window opened I felt a breeze and I felt a spirit transmitted from the window, over the garden, like a turbo-charged force. It was overwhelming. Except for the wafer, it was like the Jewish religion. Never had anything like that happened to me. I felt one with everyone. Later I realized my hyperemotional state might have had a lot to do with all the drugs I was taking.

We then went into another room, with another priest and a young seminarian. Then the Pope came in and our guide introduced him to me. He said, "May God bless your family," and he gave us each a plastic rosary. I went and kissed his ring, but he started walking away before I could say, "Holy Father, please pray for me." Everything became emotion. I wanted a picture alone with him but you're not allowed to take your own picture. The Vatican staff takes care of that. As he walked away, Christina ran up to him and put her arm on his shoulder. She asked him to pray for me. That girl has spunk.

Then we returned to the boat. Just as I was about to be helped up the gangplank, my pants fell down, probably because I had lost so much weight. I was just standing there in the sunshine in my boxer shorts with my pants around my ankles grinning at everyone. Everyone on the boat howled with laughter. I always said that if anyone was willing to drop his pants, it was me.

◆ ◆ ◆

My family decided to end the tour in Naples. It was too much. We couldn't go to Israel. I am afraid that the cancer is spreading. The Monday after we returned, I went for an MRI. It was good news. The tumor had not spread. That was a huge relief. It was as though I've been given another chance.

The Aish Hatorah arranged a hookup so I could speak at the awards ceremony at the Knesset on the Thursday. I feel I'm on the roller coaster again. Going up.

Life is strange. The nurse who's caring for me, Barbara Rose, is the same nurse Patty Watt had for several years when she was fighting breast cancer. It's been a difficult week. I went to see *Jolson*, the musical, again with my family. It was exhausting. Everything seems difficult. Walking, seeing, eating. I don't want to be in a wheelchair, and I don't want to be dead. I feel like a fuckup. I'm lying here in a hospital room getting my chemo and I feel like a total fuckup. I don't have a place. I don't want to go back to the company. But there's nothing else right now. I'm not used to being in limbo. I want to be alive when I die.

By the end of September, though, I was getting better movement in my arm and right hand. I've got a physiotherapist working with me now and two registered nurses stay with me around the clock. I've started my program of chemo plus my wonder drug. My appetite is coming back, in small doses, and I'm starting to sleep more normally. Sometimes you get a fleeting glimpse of hope that you have to hang on to. Today I had a visit from a guy who was diagnosed with the same kind of tumor six years ago. His surgery left him paralyzed on one side. Then he went to Israel to see a doctor. He's been okay ever since. So I sent my medical records over to him to take a look at.

Yesterday I cheered myself up by buying Nancy a little gift, a Bentley convertible. I wanted to surprise her. It's the same green as my Ferrari. Went out in the afternoon for the first time in four weeks. I had to do something to make myself feel good. It worked.

Lawrie Bloomberg came over the other night. He thinks I could get a lot more money for Cott. But the only reason I would sell it would be to let me do something creative again. It never occurred to me to sell it over the past two years. It was more than an important possession. It's where I went every morning. It's what I did. It wasn't as if I had twenty businesses. Cott was it. Now I want to be creative again.

Today a great thing happened. An article ran in *The Globe and Mail* about entrepreneurs who turn failure into success. And there I was, my picture between Donald Trump and Peter Munk, who runs the gold company Barrick. The head was "Entrepreneurs Ban the F-Word: Failure." It was about serial successes. The first sentence sums up my philosophy: "Entrepreneurs never fail, they just have learning experiences." That's the point. Most journalists don't understand that. That there are no red lights, only green.

My niece Sara wrote an essay for her Grade 6 class titled "My Hero." It was about me. Jesse came to the hospital with Stacey to see me. He made me a beautiful picture filled with hugs and kisses.

By the first week of October I felt the wonder drug, the SRT 101 immune booster, kicking in. I feel fantastic. My face has changed since yesterday. My eyes look exactly the way they did before I was sick. I feel the same way I did after surgery. I need to establish a routine. That's my next challenge. Warren tells me I'm getting better. What I want to know is when I will walk again. Next week I'm going to have an intake valve put in my chest, which means I won't have to have IV. It's a matter of time before the drug is made legal. The fact that I made a $5-million commitment to the foundation probably influenced the fact they're giving this to me. It all rolls the wheel.

The roller coaster seems to be speeding up. Great highs, then great lows, then highs again. Right now there's a lot of buzz about Cott. The papers are writing that it might be up for sale. Analysts are talking about it being worth $20 a share. Finally Cott is being appreciated for what it has done.

Then I found out the chairman of Coca-Cola, Robert Goizueta, died on Sunday. He was sixty-five years old. He was diagnosed with lung cancer in September and lived about six weeks. That really depressed me, even though his cancer was different from mine. I'm going on five months with this thing.

231

On October 19 I had a tenth-anniversary-of-the-stock-market-crash seizure in the evening. Lucky for me, Danny Silver and Warren Mason were both at my house so they helped me through it. Who knows how this will all turn out? At the end of October, they hooked me up to a feeding tube. I wasn't eating enough. I'm a mess. My arms are bruised with the IV. You never know how far from death you are. We'll see how close or far I am.

When I got the results of my MRI in the first week of November, it looked like the tumor had shrunk about 10 per cent from my last MRI in August. My family was ecstatic about that. They were ready to throw a party. There still is hope.

That high was followed by a mysterious infection that forced me into hospital. I needed two blood transfusions. I didn't want to come home, but everyone forced me. About ten minutes after I came through the door, I had another a seizure, my biggest yet. Things seem tough right now. But my eyes still look good.

The Globe and Mail business magazine ran a story about Cott. Dave Nichol was interviewed for it and he showed real class. He said he took on a job that wasn't right for him and he was sorry about what happened. You've got to be a big man to do that. It changed my opinion of him. Now I'm worried about him. But I never met a guy who believed in excellence the way he did. The Yiddish term for what he is is *boulvan*. I'm lonely now. Imagine how he must feel.

I have a great medical team helping me through this: Warren Mason, Danny Silver, Barry Borden. I would have been dead without them. I've been very lucky. These guys spend a tremendous amount of time with me. In October I hired Warren to be the medical director of the foundation. We're lining up some terrific people for the board.

It's a real fight. It's not just one thing. It's always something else. And yet I'm alive. I'll be around for another shot. What I thought I'd put up with I'm putting up ten times more to be alive, to see my grandchildren. My kids have been fantastic. They've been with me every day. There's nothing right now that's more important than my family.

Maybe there was no other way to sit and talk to Nancy. I probably didn't talk with her for two hours straight in two years. I was always in the middle of chaos. I was always worried about one thing or another. Now she's finding out really more about what's in my head than she's found out in thirty years living with me. It wasn't until my illness that I realized a lot about what Nancy has had to deal with over the years. It wasn't just the long hours, or the days away. The price that she has had to pay was higher in many ways than the price I ever paid.

She's been my real business partner for thirty years, and I never appreciated that until now. She's been with me every step. Sitting in the car when I catered that big party for Rolls-Royce. Giving birth to Clarke when I was at an opening of Curly Joe's. Serving pizza at Man and His World. It was hard for her, really hard, going through these different periods of my life—the wild and woolly days when I used to come home at three o'clock in the morning. Those were tough times for her, home all day with the kids. She was left dealing with Clarke's illness while I was running back and forth. Then during the time that she had available she'd help me at work.

She also was great at creating a social life for us. Over the years, we tended to socialize with people I did business with. Not for business reasons but because we genuinely liked these people. Sometimes the relationships didn't last. My attitude "go big or go home" could break up friendships. There was no room for compromise. And if there was a falling-out, which happened from time to time, Nancy lost people who were important to her. She was close to people at Financial Trustco. We had a lot of friends in Calgary. Nancy didn't want to move to Toronto, but she did. Some people might think that she's had the perfect life, with the beautiful house and the trips and the fancy jewellery. But deep down she likes simple things.

For the first time she told me about how afraid she was of being alone. Nancy is vivacious and remarkably easy to get along with. Everyone who knows her loves her. But it also means that she doesn't show her real pain. She deserves more than any executive with the company. My brothers have made a fortune. So have the shareholders. Where is Nancy's contribution acknowledged? Without her, I couldn't have done what I did. I wish I had known that earlier.

◆ ◆ ◆

For the last year, before I even knew I had this thing, I felt that it would be great if Nancy could find something new to do. So she took over running our charitable foundation, even though it wasn't a whole lot, maybe a few hundred thousand dollars a year. Now she's become really involved with the foundation. I even wanted her name on it. It was registered as the Gerry and Nancy Pencer Brain Trust in the middle of August. The Watt Group came up with a logo that looks like a cartoon of me. I wanted it to be fun.

In November, Nancy and Holly went to Washington to participate in Brain Tumor Awareness Week, sponsored by the North American Brain Tumor Coalition. Ted Kennedy spoke at the lunch about his son Teddy who was diagnosed with cancer when he was twelve and he had a 15 per cent chance of survival.

Then he had an experimental protocol. Today he has a three-year-old and another child on the way.

My Holly spoke at the rally outside Capitol Hill. What she said really touched me. "There is a reason my father got this disease," she said. "It's because he's a fighter and he will use his illness to make a difference in the lives of those who suffer from it. If his past track record is any indication, the world of brain tumors will never be the same again."

The Princess Margaret Hospital has given us half of the eighteenth floor to set up the foundation. I plan to have my office in there, to give me a new start. Maybe I'll do something else later. Who knows? I feel as if I've been given another mission. The other day I found out that the government won't give MRIs to the average person who's been diagnosed with what I have. It's too expensive. They think these people don't have enough time in front of them to justify the expense. I want the thinking about this disease to get away from the hard and professional and more toward people and relationships. I want to help all of these people who have been dehumanized because they've been given a death sentence. The government has got to be accountable. I want to have a press conference and introduce a guy who was turned down for an MRI. I want to tell his story. That should shake things up a bit.

I've never been on a roller coaster like this one. One day an MRI shows that the tumor is in remission. Then two days later you find out you have another problem. I feel so vulnerable. I even need people to help me sip a cup of tea.

What frightens me is being fully aware of what's going on but not being able to do anything about it. Yet what I've learned is that you endure these things and are willing to endure more. Sometimes I ask myself how many times I'm going to have to go up to the punching bag. I was thinking of selling Gerry Pencer "cope certificates." It would help people fight, to never give up.

I might be the first guy to fake this out. I haven't figured out yet how I'm going to win this one. I won't know until I do. But I'm telling everyone I'm going to write a sequel to this book in a year or two. Do I know I'm going to do it? No. But I never do. The only thing I know is that I'm ready for the next ride. And I'll do anything to be on it. And that I'm a really lucky guy. People think I'm joking about this, but I'm not. I'm the luckiest guy in the world.

Epilogue

This narrative ends in the fall of 1997, as Gerry entered the final stages of his final battle. A few months later, on February 3, 1998, a cold and miserable winter evening in Toronto, my beloved husband finally succumbed to the only adversary he could not overcome. I said goodbye to my rock of Gibraltar, my mentor and the love of my life. With our children and me holding and kissing him, singing his favourite songs to him and telling him how much we loved him, we watched him take his last breath. He was finally at peace.

Gerry left me and all who knew and loved him with so much of himself. He taught us about courage and dignity and living life to its fullest. And about compassion and conviction and laughter. And he taught me to reach for the stars. "You can do anything you want to do," he would say to me. "If you don't aim for the best in life, you don't have a chance."

Gerry's funeral, attended by a "standing room only" crowd (which included friends and colleagues we hadn't seen in decades), was very much a celebration of his life, as opposed to a mourning of his death, just as Gerry would have wanted. The eulogies were delivered by my daughter Holly, my son-in-law David and my brother Steve. They summed him up with just the right balance of gravity and levity. He would have liked that, too. Steve spoke for all of us when he said, "in the words of the old pop tune, Gerry was 'here for a good time, not a long time.' And what a good time it was."

In the summer of 1998, our family sold a majority of our

holdings in Cott to Thomas H. Lee & Company, a Boston based leveraged buy-out firm. For the first time since its inception, there were no Pencers on Cott's management team.

Our strongest commitment to Gerry's memory was now to fulfill his vision of establishing a Centre of Excellence at Toronto's Princess Margaret Hospital. It was with enormous pride and satisfaction that the Gerry and Nancy Pencer Brain Tumor Centre officially opened its doors to patients and families on November 18, 1998. Holly is the centre's executive director and David is the chairman of the advisory board. Gerry's dream was to raise awareness about brain tumors and to raise funds on behalf of the Centre. Hanging in the conference room are the boxing gloves that Gerry wore to the Cott 1997 annual meeting. They are there to inspire patients in their fight against the disease that has brought them to the Centre.

The Centre is dedicated to making a difference in the lives of patients and their families who live everyday with brain tumors. The success of the Centre can be measured by the positive impact that it has had on those who have come in for treatment, support, education, or just to take a look around. The Brain Trust and Centre advisory boards include Gerry's family, his close friends and many of Toronto's pre-eminent cancer researchers.

Some might think that Gerry's roller coaster ride came to a halting stop on the day that he died, but for us, his family and those who were fortunate enough to know Gerry, he'll always be with us. He would encourage us to hang on, enjoy the thrill of the ride, and never give up. Gerry wanted his legacy to be the inspiration that others can take, not from the way he died, but from the way he lived. We won't ever forget you, Gerry.

Rest in peace my love,

Nancy

Index

240